To Steve—
Happy Fathers Day
With all my love
Carol

SUPERSONIC
SAINTS

SUPERSONIC
SAINTS

THRILLING STORIES FROM LDS PILOTS

COMPILED BY

JOHN BYTHEWAY

ILLUSTRATIONS BY CHAD S. BAILEY

ᴧᴧ®

DESERET BOOK
SALT LAKE CITY, UTAH

Pencil drawings © Chad S. Bailey (airartcsbailey.com): 11, 23, 32, 42, 50, 58, 69, 80, 90, 102, 114, 122, 132, 139, 152, 160
Technical drawings courtesy Richard Ferriere (richard.ferriere.free.fr): viii, 4, 16, 28, 38, 46, 54, 60, 86, 94, 110, 120, 128, 136, 146
Shuttle drawing courtesy NASA: 74
Cobra helicopter drawing courtesy Fotosearch: 156
All photos courtesy of the respective authors

Library of Congress Cataloging-in-Publication Data

Supersonic Saints : thrilling stories from LDS pilots / compiled by John Bytheway.
   p. cm.
  ISBN-13: 978-1-59038-747-4 (hardback : alk. paper)
  1. Church of Jesus Christ of Latter-day Saints—Biography.
2. Mormon Church—Biography. 3. Air pilots—Anecdotes. 4.Air pilots—Religious life. I. Bytheway, John, 1962–
  BX8678.A475 2007
  289.3092'273—dc22
  [B]
                         2007002449

Printed in the United States of America
Worzalla Publishing Co., Stevens Point, WI

10 9 8 7 6 5 4 3 2 1

CONTENTS

Introduction 1
John Bytheway

Chapter One 5
The Voice of the Spirit at 500 Knots
Thales A. "Tad" Derrick

Chapter Two 17
The Little Green Light
David M. Nelson

Chapter Three 29
The Rescue
Ralph S. Hansen

Chapter Four 39
I Saw a Small Hole in the Clouds
William T. Garner

Chapter Five 47
Fly Off My Wing—I'll Stay with You
David M. Nelson

CONTENTS

Chapter Six 55
Thunderbirds to South America
Leonard Moon

Chapter Seven 61
They're There Every Time
Gil Bertelson

Chapter Eight 75
If Ye Are Prepared Ye Shall Not Fear
Rick Searfoss

Chapter Nine 87
Almost Shot Down
Leonard Moon

Chapter Ten 95
A Tornado in the Cockpit
Thales A. "Tad" Derrick

Chapter Eleven 111
Distinguished Flying Cross
Oscar R. "Ron" Adams

Chapter Twelve 121
You Never Know When Someone Is Listening
William Spencer

Chapter Thirteen 129
Unsafe Gear Indicator
Thomas W. McKnight

Chapter Fourteen 137
Silver Star
Oscar R. "Ron" Adams

CONTENTS

Chapter Fifteen 147
Vertigo
Thomas W. McKnight

Chapter Sixteen 157
Stand in Your Place and Trust God
to Watch Over You
David Stock

Index 173

F-16 FIGHTING FALCON

INTRODUCTION

JOHN BYTHEWAY

Airplanes have been a fascination of mine since before I could walk. When I was in grade school, anytime an airplane flew overhead, I had to stop my kick ball game and look up. My parents used to take me to the observation area at the Salt Lake airport for my birthday. Since this book is in your hands, my guess is that you may have the same fascination.

When I began high school, my plan was to go on a mission for The Church of Jesus Christ of Latter-day Saints, come home, and fly fighter jets. I didn't want to go to war; I just wanted to fly something grossly overpowered. One day, while enjoying a game of bowling with some friends, I noticed the little lighted number 1 at the end of the lane, and it didn't look right. It looked like 11. I squinted, I tried to focus, I rubbed my eyes, but there was no way of getting around it. My vision was *not* 20/20. The optometrist told me I had astigmatism. There went my military career and my boyhood dream to see the words *Captain John G. Bytheway* stenciled proudly beneath an F-16 canopy. I was heartbroken. Shortly thereafter, I remember driving past Hill Air Force Base on I-15 and watching through the sunroof a couple of fighter jets prepare for approach. I almost cried right there in the car. Oh well. My eyes were bad, and my life would have to take another path.

After my mission, one of my college roommates, Tom McKnight (see chapters 13 and 15), persuaded me to go to the Provo airport and take a lesson or two. I had already completed ground school (as a 16-year-old), so I didn't need a lot of preparation. To make a long story short, I finally soloed in a Cessna 152. A far cry from the F-16 I dreamed of, but it was still one of the most thrilling moments of my life.

Supersonic Saints is the book I wish I had owned during those years. I would have read it until I wore it out. I love these airplanes, and after compiling these stories, I love these pilots, too. No one wants to go to war, as these pilots will tell you. But they are to be honored for answering the call of their country and striving to defend the cause of freedom around the world.

2

Not all of the airplanes described in this book are supersonic, but the stories sure are—they will raise your heart rate, tighten your muscles, and most important, lift your spirit. As an airplane enthusiast and a Latter-day Saint, I am very excited to share these stories with you. So sit back, get comfortable, and buckle up—you're about to go for a great ride.

F-100 SUPER SABRE

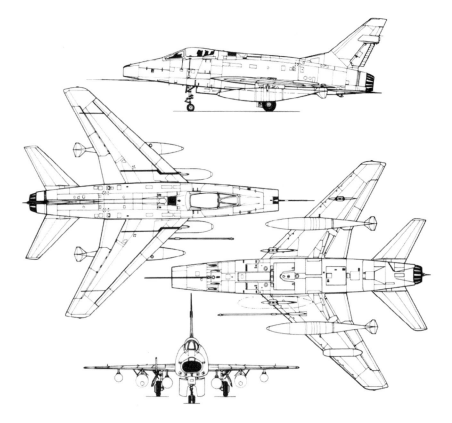

CHAPTER ONE

THE VOICE OF THE SPIRIT AT 500 KNOTS

THALES A. "TAD" DERRICK

The 481st Tactical Fighter Squadron of the United States Air Force, to which I was assigned, was deployed to Vietnam in June 1965. This was one of the first full-squadron deployments of the war, even though individual pilots had been involved as advisors to the South Vietnamese Air Force for years. My assignment was as assistant operations officer and mission scheduling officer. My main job was to match pilots with planes and combat missions. I also flew an equal share of combat missions with the rest of the squadron pilots. At the time, I was a senior captain and had the second highest amount of flying time (about 2,400 hours) in our unit aircraft, the F-100D Super Sabre.

We used to say that "every day was Wednesday," because we flew missions 24/7, to use today's jargon. It didn't matter what day it was because they all were pretty much alike. It's that way in combat. Sundays were favorite days for the enemy to ambush our ground troops, and we flew as much on the Sabbath as on any other day. We learned quickly that we needed the Sabbath (which was made for man; see Mark 2:27), but it was hard to arrange very often.

One day, I scheduled myself to lead a flight of four F-100Ds against an emplacement of Viet Cong troops that were shelling and attacking the U.S. Army and South Vietnamese Army forces in the IV Corp Area, the Mekong Delta of South Vietnam. My number four pilot was Captain John Parker. He was not a regular 481st pilot but had been recently assigned to help fill the ranks because we were flying so many combat missions.

I conducted the regular preflight briefing, which outlined our target attack tactics for dive bombing using 750 general purpose bombs. We learned from the intelligence officer, First Lieutenant Tom Lowe, that we could expect fairly heavy automatic weapons fire from the Viet Cong. Because this was Captain Parker's first combat mission, I emphasized that we would vary our attack headings (what nonpilots might call angle of approach), that Parker should remember to "jink" his aircraft on the beginning of the dive, stabilizing just before bomb release, and then jink again on the pull-off from the target. (Jinking is the unpredictable moving of the aircraft in all directions: up, down, right, or left in a random pattern so that ground gunners cannot predict the place the aircraft will be next and thus fire so that the aircraft "runs into" the bullets.)

Soon we were on our way to the target. The weather was clear. This was both good and bad. It meant we would have a clear view of the target area, but the ground gunners would also have a clear view of our F-100Ds. I contacted our forward air controller (FAC), who was our link with the friendly forces on the ground. Our FAC was airborne in a small L-19 Bird Dog aircraft to assess the best location for our bombs and get current locations of the friendly forces. He relayed all this information to our four fighters as we approached the target. He then shot a smoke rocket for a reference point and told us that the "bad guys" were along a small canal that was connected to a jungle forest on the north. He suggested we bomb the north bank of the canal and the adjacent forest where the main concentration of enemy forces was located. I led the attack and dropped two 750s. They hit the desired area. The number two aircraft attacked from a slightly different heading, and number three adjusted his attack to again confuse enemy gunners.

I was setting up for my second attack when I noticed that Captain Parker was playing follow the leader behind number three. He was not jinking, either. Just as I punched my radio button to say, "Jink, Number Four," I saw pieces of metal and fluid coming from his aircraft. He had been hit by ground fire. He pulled out of his dive and began climbing for altitude.

Directing numbers two and three to continue the attack, I went into afterburner and quickly caught up with John's aircraft. He had a large hole in the right wing and was losing fuel rapidly from that wing tank. He was also losing hydraulic fluid. His radio was shot out, and we had to communicate by hand signals (kind of like a pilot's one-handed American Sign Language). John indicated he had lost one hydraulic flight control system and that other warning and caution lights were on. I communicated that I would lead him home and that we would go out past the South Vietnam shoreline in case he had to eject. The water was a more friendly place than the VC-infested jungle.

I made radio contact with our tactical air control center and told them I was bringing home a badly damaged number four. The center picked us up on radar.

About that time, we were passing over the southern-most channel of the Mekong River where it empties into the South China Sea. We were near the town of Long Phu. As I looked to my right to check on John, I noticed that he was pointing frantically to his right wing. I thought, *Oh, he's noticed the big fuel leak.* But I pulled my aircraft up slightly to look over the top of his plane and saw that his right wing was totally engulfed in flames.

He signaled that he was going to eject. I moved left to give him lots of room.

Fooom! Off came the canopy, followed immediately by the ejection seat and John strapped to it. He separated from the seat cleanly, and his parachute opened automatically. A nice, fully blossomed chute. As I circled John, he signaled he was OK, and he deployed his life preservers and life raft because he was definitely going "in the drink."

Alerting the tactical air control center that number four had ejected, I requested a rescue helicopter "on the double." They said they'd get working on the problem.

The water that leaves the Mekong River at most times of the year is kind of a muddy yellow. It was this color when John hit the water with his yellow life raft and became immediately invisible. Before his parachute sank, I marked the spot with reference to some landmarks on the coast and circled as I pleaded with the center for the helicopter. It was then I noticed THE BOATS!

There were four good-sized, sail-powered fishing boats about 90 degrees apart around the circle I was making. John was in the center of the circle. Suddenly, I noticed that all the boats had altered course and were heading for the center of the circle and John. Who were these people? Innocent fishermen or Viet Cong running guns up or down the river? I didn't want them messing with John either way! I called the center and asked if they had any ideas about how to handle the boat issue. They came back with an unhelpful "Use your own discretion."

I assessed my options. I had two 750-pound bombs left. One bomb would more than destroy one boat, so two boats could be sunk with bombs. I still had a full load of 800 rounds of 20 millimeter high-explosive shells that could be spit out of four cannons at a rate of 1,500 rounds per minute per gun. The guns could make kindling wood out of the other two boats. But what if they were innocent fishermen?

I prayed, *"Father, I want to protect John from the*

enemy, but I don't want to kill innocent fishermen. What shall I do?

I needed an answer immediately, and it came immediately. The still, small voice said, *"You don't need to destroy them. You can scare them into stopping."*

I remember smiling to myself. A fighter plane can be pretty intimidating without firing a shot.

I pushed the throttle up full bore, and the aircraft accelerated quickly to 500 knots (approximately 575 mph). I dropped down just above the ocean, using the height of the mast on the nearest boat for gauging my

distance above the water. I ran at the boat a little lower than mast height, and just as I got to the boat, I pulled up abruptly and lit the afterburner. KA-BOOM! I don't know if I blew the sail down with jet-wash or if the fishermen dropped the sail. The boat was still afloat, but it had stopped still in the water. I used the same tactic on the other three boats. All sat motionless. Whew! A prayer of thanks: *I thank Thee, Father! That was great!*

Now, where was that helicopter? I was getting low on fuel. The center indicated that a helicopter had me in sight. I got the chopper pilot on the radio and said that the downed pilot was in the center of my circle. He acknowledged and said he would begin a low-level sweep of the circle center. Soon he spotted John bobbing around in his life raft.

At that point, the chopper pilot said he would take over the rescue and not to worry about the fishing boats. He was an armed "Huey" and could stand them off if things got ugly.

I acknowledged and boogied for home base.

The story doesn't end there, though. Because the UH-I Huey was a gunship, it didn't carry standard rescue equipment. It didn't have a sling to drop to the pilot. In fact, it didn't even have a rope. The chopper pilot knew something about air-to-sea pickup, however, and motioned for John to get out of his raft and into the water, because chopper rotor-wash blows a life raft away anytime the chopper tries to move in close.

The plan: Get the chopper down close and have one of the gunners lean over and pull John into the chopper.

The reality: John was 6'2" and 190-plus pounds dry. The biggest gunner was 5'6" and 140 pounds soaking wet.

The laws of physics apply: "There ain't no way gunner is going to pull pilot into chopper."

Conference in the chopper cockpit. Hmmm. OK. The sea is rolling in two- to three-foot gentle swells with about 80 feet between swells. The chopper pilot decides that if he times it just right, he can "land the chopper in the water" deep enough for John to scramble up on the skid and then pull up before the next swell washes through the open doors on both sides.

He does it. John does it, and it's up, up, and away! (The chopper pilot received a well-deserved medal for the rescue.)

When John returned to the base at Tan Son Nhut

and was cleared by the flight surgeon, I gave him a hug and told him not to forget to jink next time. He never forgot.

And neither did I forget the generous blessing of a loving Father for sending the message of the Spirit to me at 500 knots.

PILOT'S BIOGRAPHY

Rank and branch of service: lieutenant colonel, United States
   Air Force, retired

Call sign: Meteor

Hometowns: Salt Lake City and St. George, Utah (since 1974)

Family: married to Willa Nita Brooks; five children; 22 grandchildren

Church callings: formerly served as bishop, stake president, and
   president of Pennsylvania Pittsburgh Mission, 1992–95;
   currently serves as Gospel Doctrine teacher

Current occupation: retired

Hobbies: flying his own airplane, growing fruit trees and gar-
   dening, spending time with grandchildren

Awards and recognitions: Distinguished Flying Cross, Air Medal
   (five), Meritorious Service (three), among others

Tad Derrick (right) and the F-100
"Mormon Meteor"

T-37 DRAGONFLY

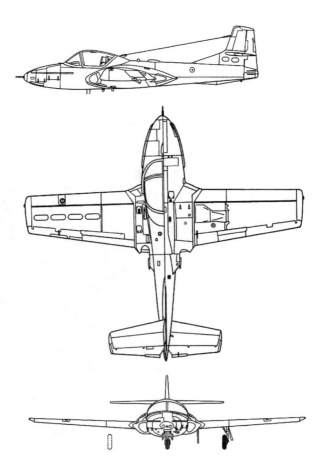

CHAPTER TWO

THE LITTLE GREEN LIGHT

DAVID M. NELSON

The first jet airplane I ever flew was the T-37 during undergraduate pilot training. I remember being impressed during training that the United States Air Force could train a pilot so thoroughly in only a few months in normal procedures, basic maneuvers, instrument flying, and emergency procedures. In retrospect, I am even more in awe of the process of taking young civilians off the street and in a short time converting them into fledgling aviators with newly acquired skills and decision-making abilities.

The process was an exciting one. First, there were about three weeks of ground school. We were issued our first flight suits, pilot watches, and pilot sunglasses. Simulator training followed. Then our first flights came. Less than a month after our first flight, we were prepared for our initial solo flights in our own jet airplanes, one of the most exciting flights for a novice military pilot. I went out for a flight with the instructor just to practice a few takeoffs and landings. Then we landed and shut down the engine on his side. After a quick "Be careful," he climbed out. I started the engine back up, closed the canopy, and taxied off to my personal epic of flight. That was 23 years ago.

Aerobatics and spin training followed. We progressed through instrument and cross-country and low-level flights. Simulator training got more intense with engine failures, hydraulic malfunctions, fires, radio outages, navigation aid failures, and so on. With the passage of time, my confidence grew. Due to the high-quality training, I began to believe that I could handle anything the airplane could throw at me. We would launch the T-37 into violent spins and then accomplish a multistep recovery procedure. "Stinking excellent!" one instructor exclaimed after one of my spin recoveries. We became masters of the T-37 aircraft.

Finally, the last phase of training arrived: Formation. We had all seen it done. We all thought it looked fun and believed we could do it. We had had ground school training on formation flying. We were scheduled for formation flights and were briefed for the sequence of events we would follow on the ground and in the air—

almost choreographing every move between the two airplanes and crews in our formation. The instructor demonstrated a formation takeoff, maintaining close separation from brake release for takeoff through gear retraction, and then "tucking it in" really tight to about three feet of wingtip separation. It looked effortless. I was soon to find out it would not be effortless for me.

When I arrived at a safe training altitude, the instructor barked that I would soon have the controls in my hand and be responsible for maintaining the separation he seemed to have no trouble holding. "Put your hands on the stick and throttles and follow my inputs," he said.

I felt the stick moving as the instructor made subtle motions to keep our airplane glued to the wing of the lead airplane, but it didn't make any sense why he made the movements that he made. It appeared that the instructor made the control inputs without even thinking about them. They just happened. I felt the throttles move smoothly up and back to maintain the fore and aft position, but again I felt incapable of executing similar, effective inputs. I felt like a dog watching TV—it was interesting, but it made absolutely no sense.

Then the instructor muttered, "You have the

airplane," at which point he released the controls and I was flying on the wing of another jet airplane. There was no feeling of accomplishment, glee, or pride. On the contrary, great beads of sweat broke out on my forehead. My grip on the stick tightened until I thought it would be crushed in my grasp. I couldn't think of both the stick and the throttle at the same time, so as I made stick corrections to fix in-and-out or up-and-down position errors, the throttles were motionless and great fore-aft errors resulted.

When I took the airplane for the first time, I corrected a slight up error with too much "down stick"—OOPS—now "up stick" to fix that. OH! Too much again. Even more down stick now—AHHH, too much again. Then up-down-Up-Down—UP—DOWN. Farther and farther we would oscillate from the smooth flight path my instructor had so effortlessly maintained on the wing of the lead aircraft. In addition to the wild up-down variations, a sort of self-preservation instinct began to act in such a way that a lateral separation began to build between the two airplanes. My subconscious said, *If I'm going to flail around up and down like this, at least I'll do it far away from this other airplane so we won't hit.*

As if I didn't have my hands full enough, the

instructor asked in feigned wonder, "Why are we falling behind?" It was because in all my thinking about the necessary stick inputs, the throttle inputs required to keep us close to lead were abandoned. So up came the throttles, up and down went the stick, farther and farther we got from lead.

"I've got the airplane," the instructor calmly stated as he took the stick and throttle and damped my oscillations, smoothly gliding up to lead, setting me up for another try. I wonder if there was a grin behind the oxygen mask of my instructor. I imagined him over in the other seat thinking, *So, you thought you were the master of the T-37, did you?*

It was a rough start to a challenging phase of training, but in a short time, to our astonishment, we mastered formation flying, too. Within a few flights, we were able to tuck it in and stay with the flight lead, even through some mild maneuvers. This was something I would not have thought possible on that first formation flight. But the instructor pilots had seen the transformation happen in student pilots before and had every confidence that our class would be similarly successful. They patiently passed on the secrets of their years of experience. Humbled by our experience (or lack thereof), we listened. At the end of training, the instructors presented me with the award for being the best formation pilot in our 40-man class. Months later, the skills they passed to us in formation flying paid off.

The mission began as a practice scramble from the alert facility at Holloman AFB, New Mexico. Our two F-15 fighter planes blasted off in full afterburner and climbed rapidly to the en route altitude. We flew in loose formation to the working area and practiced intercepting each other for about an hour. One of us would simulate being a target while the other would direct his radar and accept vectors to an intercept from a remote controlling agency that kept watch over the borders of the country.

We reached "bingo fuel," meaning it was time to return to the base. What we didn't know was that while we were training, a great thunderstorm had built over the mountains and separated us from our home base. Lower altitude stratus clouds masked the billowing storm from our view. As we entered the light weather on the edge of the storm, my flight lead rocked his wings side to side, the signal to tighten up the formation. I complied by sliding in to close formation, holding about three feet of wingtip separation. I maintained steady position by lining up the anti-collision light on the lead's airplane with his blade antenna and holding

it there with throttle and stick corrections—just as we had been taught in training.

The weather thickened, and the turbulence increased. Jostling from the turbulence made it more difficult to stay in the proper position. Thickening clouds began to challenge my view of the flight lead's airplane. Occasionally there was a dense area of cloud that would completely obscure the lead aircraft for a fraction of a second, but we would fly out the other side before needing to react with a turn away. I thought of my "lost wingman" procedure—a planned maneuver that a wingman makes if he loses sight of the flight lead. The occasional dense areas of cloud became more and more frequent until thick and dark clouds surrounded our formation, our headsets crackled with the static of nearby lightning, and our airplanes were shaken by powerful up and down drafts from the storm.

Soon worsening circumstances forced me to struggle to maintain position, and of necessity I moved to the "weather position," which is slightly aft and much closer to the lead aircraft—the wings actually overlap by several feet. Much of the time I could see enough of the lead airplane to make out the cockpit and see my flight lead's helmeted head inside the transparent canopy. He would glance at me now and then to make sure I was still there.

But in the most challenging times, I could not see that far. I lost sight of the cockpit area of his airplane. I lost sight of the tails. I lost sight of the antenna I used to maintain the proper position. The big gray fighter plane blended in with the grim, gray storm cloud more thoroughly than I had ever imagined possible. All I could see was the green wingtip light at what seemed like inches from my eyes. It was the only visible part of the aircraft that was my leader and provided me the direction home. There was no time for occasional looks inside to my cockpit gauges or for any other distraction. All my attention was focused on that last remaining particle of the flight lead's airplane—the little green light.

My flight lead tried to be considerate. He attempted to avoid maneuvering at all, and when he had to maneuver, he did so very gently so as to simplify my task of following him. I don't remember blinking during the worst of the episode. I don't remember any of the control inputs that my left hand made with the throttle or my right hand made with the stick. There was no time to think about what the control inputs should be. They just happened. The inputs were a product of hours and hours of training and practice flying in tight formation on my flight lead's wing. Without that training and practice, I would have been easily lost.

Onward we plowed through the dense weather and powerful turbulence. But finally the sky began to lighten. I was able to loosen up in the formation. The blood returned to my fingers. The challenging part of the thunderstorm had been overcome. After a few minutes, we broke out of the clouds into clear air at around 10,000 feet. Finally able to relax, I remember looking around to see where we were. The long runways of the base stretched out at our 2 o'clock a few miles away. We were home.

PILOT'S BIOGRAPHY

Rank and branch of service: lieutenant colonel, United States
  Air Force, retired

Call sign: Doc

Hometown: McLean, Virginia

Full-time mission: Ohio Columbus

Family: married to Rain Jackson; five children

Church callings: formerly served as bishop, high councilor, and
  counselor in bishoprics and branch presidencies; currently
  serves as high priest group leader

Current occupation: F-35 test pilot for an aeronautics company

Hobbies: Church and family, cars, astronomy, radio-controlled
  airplanes

Awards and recognitions: Eagle Scout, distinguished graduate
  from United States Air Force Test Pilot School; A1AA Tester
  of the Year award, 2001

Dave Nelson with the F-22 Raptor

A-10 THUNDERBOLT II

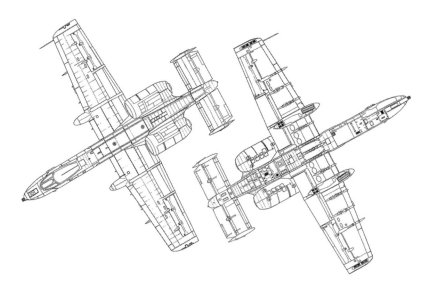

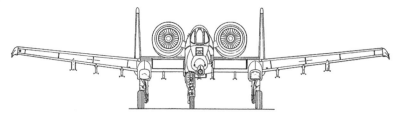

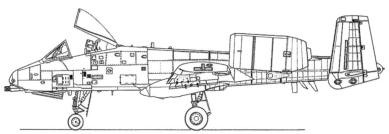

CHAPTER THREE

THE RESCUE

RALPH S. HANSEN

One night in 1996 I was flying in a two-ship of A-10s supporting a large United States Army exercise south of Fairbanks, Alaska. We had spent the evening working with an army Special Forces team, and even though the weather wasn't particularly good, the mission had been very successful. I was pretty pleased with the way things had gone and was looking forward to landing and going home after a long day. I had no way of knowing that those plans were about to be interrupted in a dramatic fashion.

As we were leaving the bombing range to head home, I overheard a conversation on the tactical frequency about one of the United States Marine Corps F-18 pilots (who were also supporting the exercise) who had lost contact with his wingman. I didn't think much about it, because that happens occasionally at night. As my wingman and I were entering the radar landing pattern a few minutes later, we received a radio call from the forward air controller, who was still on the bombing range, asking us to come back. We had already been airborne for an hour and a half, but we immediately turned around.

After we changed back to the range frequency, it quickly became apparent that the F-18 was still missing and a full-blown search-and-rescue operation was beginning. We asked the radar controllers if he was showing up anywhere on radar—hoping that he had just lost radio contact with his flight lead—but no one had heard, seen, or had radar contact with him since that first radio call. One of the other A-10s on the range mentioned a big flash of light to the south at about that time. This particular tactics range is right at the base of the Alaska Range, with mountains as tall as 14,000 feet—not a very good place to be flying around lost in the dark. To make the situation even worse, the weather began to deteriorate rapidly.

My flight, along with the other four A-10s that were still airborne, searched for any sign of an aircraft or a crash site with our night vision goggles. We also made numerous radio calls on the emergency frequencies. By now the weather had closed in. The sky was completely overcast with intermittent snow showers, and the bases of clouds were uneven, varying between 1000 and 3000 feet.

With the low ceilings, we weren't able to get very far into the valleys because of the high mountains on every side. We tried dropping some of our large parachute-borne illumination flares, but the snow made it so hazy under the clouds that the flares didn't help much. We were able to divert an army helicopter to help, but even he couldn't make it very much farther than we could due to the heavy snowfall. By then the F-18 wingman and two of the A-10s were low on fuel and had to return to the base. The visibility was so poor and the night so dark that the four of us who were left continued to drop flares to illuminate the area for the helicopter to search. It was pretty tight quarters between the clouds and the rocks, and after scaring myself a couple of times, I realized that if we weren't careful, we would have another accident on our hands.

My wingman was now getting low on fuel, and I sent him home. The two other aircraft followed shortly thereafter. Not wanting to leave the scene, and now alone, I climbed up and dropped flares above the clouds, which allowed enough light to filter down

through the clouds to cast some light on the search area.

Despite our best efforts, the helicopter wasn't able to get within five miles of the last known location of the missing aircraft. By the time I expended my last flare, I was running on fumes and had to return to base, after being airborne for more than three hours.

Our squadron commander wanted to send a single aircraft up one more time to provide some assistance. I waited while they loaded more flares on my airplane so that I could go up to continue the search. While I was waiting, I went into the bathroom to pray. It reminded me of flying in Desert Storm, when I would go into the bathroom and pray before walking out the door to go fly combat missions. I had felt so utterly helpless on the previous flight. Here I was, a highly trained search-and-rescue pilot—as qualified as one can get for this mission—and I wasn't able to do anything. My greatest fear was that this F-18 pilot had been able to eject but was hurt too badly to communicate with us and that he was going to freeze to death on some mountainside before anyone could get to him. I prayed that if he was out there, I or someone else could find him before it was too late. By this time I had been at work for more than twelve hours and had to get a waiver just to be able to fly longer than the allowed duty day.

I finally got airborne, but the weather was too poor for me to get under the clouds at all, and I wasn't able to do much good. By now an air force rescue helicopter and two army medical evacuation helicopters had joined the search. I dropped illumination flares above the clouds to provide enough light for them to safely fly through the mountains on this pitch-black night. I had them try three different approaches to the suspected crash site, but they were blocked at every turn. The weather was just too bad. When they started talking about flying 70 feet above the ground in a driving snowstorm with visibility only one-eighth of a mile, I knew it was hopeless and called off the search. I was finally ordered to land after another two hours of providing illumination and direction to the helicopters. I landed about 1 A.M., as tired as I have ever been in an airplane. I'm sure a lot of that was the emotional strain of this particular mission.

On my way home, I finally had time to think about this rescue attempt. Dozens of people in many different locations had given their all, even risking their lives, to try to save a comrade, even though we didn't know if he was alive or dead. I personally was willing to put forth that much effort, enlisting the help of every resource available, and giving all I had to rescue someone's physical life. As I looked up at the stars, I asked myself why I hadn't been willing to put forth the same kind of effort to rescue someone's spiritual life, which is far more important. Maybe it is because the need is not so immediate or the consequences so obvious. Whatever the reason, I came to the sober realization that I need to do more in reaching out to those who are in spiritual danger as surely as this pilot was in physical danger. This mission put opportunities to do those very things, such as home teaching and sharing the gospel, in a completely different light.

I wish I could say that this story had a happy ending. The crash site was found the next day, in the exact location we had been unable to get to the night before. This highly experienced pilot had lost sight of his flight lead in the dark and bad weather and had not seen the mountains until it was too late to eject.

I learned that night that in life, as in flying, we often do not see the need for a course correction until it is too late. We try to make efforts to prevent an accident, but sometimes we just do the best we can to help in the aftermath. Sometimes that help comes in the form of providing light to the searchers, and often we need to set aside our own comfort and safety and go out into the dark and cold to rescue one who is lost or in peril. Sometimes we will be successful; other times we won't; but we must continue to do all that we can.

I have often looked back at my experience that night, so many years ago. I still wish that I could have done something to help make the story have a happy ending. But I did learn about the need to give our all to reach out to those who need us, a lesson I will never forget.

PILOT'S BIOGRAPHY

Rank and branch of service: lieutenant colonel, United States
Air Force

Call sign: Ralphie

Hometown: Gresham, Oregon

Family: married to Suzanne Stacey Hansen: six children

Church callings: formerly served as Ward Young Men's president, counselor in bishopric, and high priests group
leader; currently serves as Gospel Doctrine teacher

Current occupation: A-10 program manager, Headquarters Air
Combat Command, Langley Air Force Base, Virginia

Awards and recognitions: More than 2,000 hours in the A-10
warthog, including some 150 combat missions in Kuwait,
Iraq, Bosnia, and Afghanistan; numerous military awards,
including Defense Meritorious Service Medal and 10 Air
Medals

*Ralph Hansen with his crew chief, Tony Qualls, in front of their A-10
shortly before leaving Afghanistan*

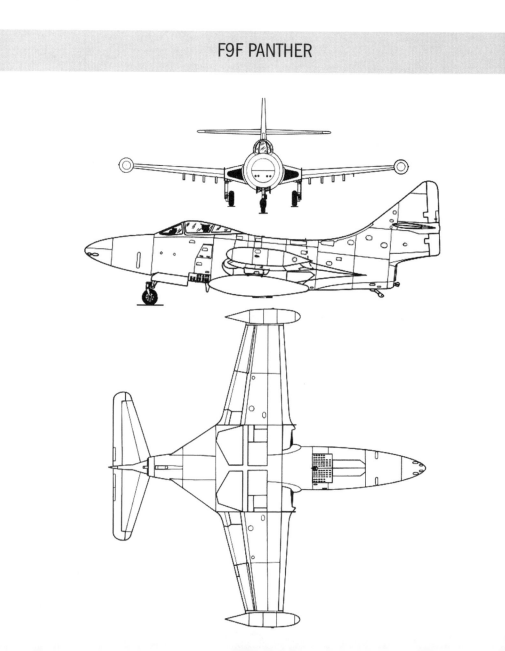

CHAPTER FOUR

I SAW A SMALL HOLE IN THE CLOUDS

WILLIAM T. GARNER

As a young fighter pilot flying F9F Panther jets with the United States Marine Corps in Korea in the winter of 1954, I was assigned to lead a four-plane division on a mission to the north. The hostilities of the Korean War had officially ended, but relations between North Korea and South Korea, and those who supported each, were unfriendly, and the situation remained tense. While we were returning to K-3, the name of our base in the south, the weather became marginal. It was apparent that we would have to fly close to the surface to remain VFR (to continue to operate on visual flight rules) and stay below the heavy clouds that were continuing to build. K-3 was on the east coast of South Korea at the mouth of a large bay and, because the terrain was mountainous, approaches to the field in poor weather were generally made over the bay. This practice permitted aircraft to fly under the clouds and keep the field in sight.

As we reached a point approximately 10 miles from the field, flying at an altitude of no more than a few hundred feet above the water, the base of the clouds abruptly dropped, and we lost virtually all visibility. I immediately began a shallow climb and informed the field by radio that we would have to be brought in on a radar ground-controlled approach (GCA). After determining that my section leader (the number three aircraft in our flight) and his wingman (the number four aircraft) had slightly less fuel than my wingman and I, and because our landing field could not accommodate more than two fighter planes at a time, I ordered my section leader to take his wingman and himself in first while my wingman and I flew courses and altitudes as directed by the GCA controller. My section leader complied. The controller directed me to change radio frequency, to assume different compass headings, and to climb to a higher altitude, all of which my wingman and I did. The situation was delicate but not particularly unusual. I had made many such approaches in the past.

Suddenly my radio transmitter ceased to function, although my receiver was still working. Because it is essential in leading a ground-controlled approach that one be able to transmit to the controller and I could not, I instructed my wingman by hand signals to assume the lead. I took up a position on his wing. The clouds were dense, and we flew in a tight formation to keep each other in sight. I expected to fly as directed by the GCA controller until the other two aircraft had been brought down safely, when it would be our turn to be guided in.

My eyes were fixed on the aircraft on which I was now flying wing when, with my peripheral vision, I was startled to see through the clouds what appeared to be a mountain looming immediately ahead and closing fast. We were about to hit it. My indicated airspeed was perhaps 350 knots (approximately 400 mph). Instinctively I snapped my control stick back and applied full power, beginning what felt like a vertical climb and completely losing sight of the other aircraft.

I continued climbing until I broke out on top of the clouds at an altitude of about 30,000 feet. Meanwhile, I heard on my radio receiver that unexpected and violent snowstorms had caused every landing field in South Korea to be closed.

I knew there was a field called K-1 near Pusan on the southern coast, about 60 miles from where I believed myself to be, and I reasoned that if I headed south, I might find that the cloud cover did not extend far beyond the southern shoreline. Perhaps I could then fly farther south to the edge of the cloud layer, descend to a few feet above sea level, and then turn back north, flying just over the water, in the direction of K-1. My fuel was nearly gone, but it seemed my only chance to survive.

To my great disappointment, as I approached what I assumed to be the coastline, I saw that the clouds continued in all directions for as far as I could see. And from my altitude, I could see for many miles. It was clear that I had insufficient fuel to reach the edge of the

cloud layer, however close it might be, and certainly not enough fuel to then descend to sea level and make it back to the coast.

I considered ejecting from my aircraft while still over land but concluded that even if I parachuted safely to the unseen mountains below, I would probably freeze to death in the blizzard then raging. I also considered waiting until I was over water to eject, but even with the protective clothing I wore and even if I could get my life raft inflated and pull myself into it, the frigid sea would not allow me to remain mobile for more than 30 minutes. For either option, rescue was unlikely. But I had to do something, so I decided to eject before reaching the sea.

At that instant, I saw just below me a small hole in the clouds and, through the hole 30,000 feet below, the landing strip of what looked like K-1. Without taking the time for a customary descent, I did a "Split-S," extended my dive brakes, and headed straight down toward the field, hoping that the hole would not close before I made it through.

My approach was not graceful, and I landed much faster than normal, blowing out both main tires in the process. But I landed, and I was alive. My fuel tanks were empty, and when I looked up to see the hole though which I had descended, it was gone. Only snow, sleet, and clouds were visible.

My wingman was not heard from again. I do not know whether he perished in the mountains or in the sea.

I have never since heard of any other small hole extending through the full thickness of clouds from just above the ground to an altitude of 30,000 feet. But the most important thing that happened to me as I was flying toward the southern coast with several minutes to contemplate what seemed to be imminent death was my anguish. It was not about dying. It was about not living well.

I recalled my past irresponsibility in my relationship with my Heavenly Father. I began to feel the sadness of one who has squandered his time and efforts and failed to use his abilities as well as he might have done, as well as he ought to have done. I felt I had wasted much of the precious gift of life. I do not recall asking for a second chance. Perhaps I felt unworthy to do so. But I do recall resolving that if a second chance were afforded me, I would live so that further regrets would not be necessary. I was blessed to receive that opportunity, and I pray that I will always remember the lesson of that experience.

PILOT'S BIOGRAPHY

Rank and branch of service: captain, United States Marine Corps, retired

Hometown: Long Beach, California

Family: married to Rochelle Ann Clark; six children; 18 grandchildren

Church callings: formerly served as bishop, high councilor, and member of a stake presidency; currently serves as stake patriarch

Current occupation: law professor; California Superior Court judge, retired

Hobbies: grandchildren, family history and temple work, videography, writing, music, sports, reading, and research

William T. Garner

F-15 EAGLE

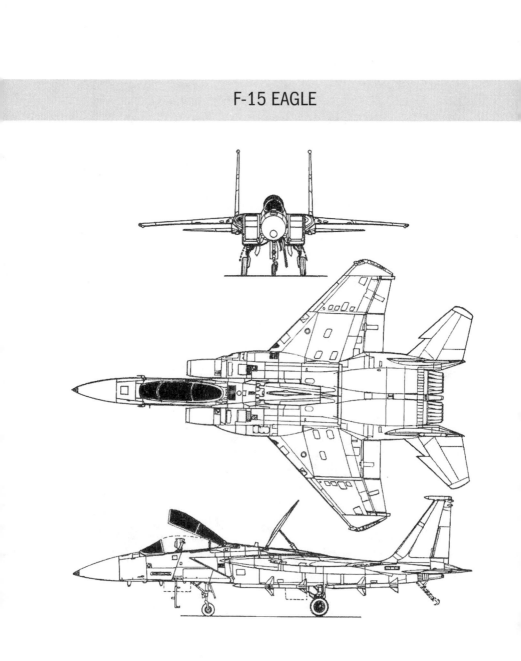

CHAPTER FIVE

FLY OFF MY WING— I'LL STAY WITH YOU

DAVID M. NELSON

I walked into the squadron building and found a crowd frozen in suspense around the operations (OPS) desk, listening to static crackling on the radio. A voice from the radio broke the silence: "I'm 15 miles south of the coastline. My engine quit . . . I'll be bailing out in 30 seconds."

The OPS desk is the heart of any fighter squadron. Ours had a radio that was always tuned to the mission frequency, allowing support folks on the ground to keep up with our in-flight events. The mission being monitored on this day was a routine aerial gunnery mission—two F-15 fighter planes were going out to practice firing their 20mm cannons at a large plywood and sheet metal target known as the Dart. The dart was towed on a long cable behind a 40-year-old single-engine F-86 Sabre jet. To increase the realism and for an added measure of safety, the F-86 would make a hard turn during gunnery practice to allow the bullets fired at the dart to pass safely behind. It was a fun mission in an intense kind of way.

The shooting was going as planned and remained safe throughout the day. Unknown to the dart tow pilot, however, the engine mounting bolts in his airplane had worked loose, and the engine had shifted on its mount, causing the compressor to come into contact with something that stopped its rotation. He quickly called, "Knock it off," the signal to all fighter pilots to stop what they're doing and mentally shift gears into a mode of increased safety. He turned toward the coastline and while turning called to the shooters that he was going to jettison the dart. This he did after the shooters called that they were clear. Jettisoning the dart reduced the amount of drag on the powerless aircraft and enabled it to glide farther.

Adjusting his pitch attitude to hold the proper glide speed, the F-86 pilot began to analyze the situation. RPM was zero—the engine wasn't turning, so unless the tachometer was lying, there would be no restart for this engine. The instruments in the cockpit that required engine power quit. The artificial horizon—the instrument that told the pilot which way was up while flying in the clouds—had quit. Without the artificial horizon, a pilot flying in clouds can easily become subject to a life-threatening condition called spatial disorientation: He can feel right side up when he is really upside down or vice versa.

There was a small airport up ahead on the coast. Maybe the F-86 pilot could land there. But a thick deck of clouds below prevented him from either seeing it or navigating to it. With no ability to find a safe landing field, or even know where he was, and with the potential of creating a hazard to the people on shore, the pilot decided that the wise thing to do would be to glide toward shore for as long as he could stay out of the clouds, then bail out, and hope he could get picked up. That's when he made his call: "I'll be bailing out in 30 seconds." As the clouds began to lick the underside of the wing on the F-86, the pilot knew it wouldn't be long before he had to leave the airplane.

Just about then the F-15 flight lead, who had been following the F-86 in its glide for shore, had a flash of insight. He called over the radio, "Don't bail out. I'm joining on your left wing." The pilot looked to his left to see the F-15 fighter plane quickly closing on him. The F-15 called, "Fly off my wing, and I'll adjust my power to stay with you."

This call made us wonder what the new plan was, but we didn't dare use precious time to ask. As we huddled around the OPS desk with puzzled looks on our faces, the flight lead called again and sent his wingman ahead—"Two," he said (that's how you address your wingman on the radio), "push it up. Go find the runway at Apalachicola [an abandoned airport with no navigation aids and a dilapidated old runway] and orbit there."

"Two" complied by lighting his afterburner and racing at just under Mach 1, penetrating the cloud layer on instruments to find the runway. The F-15 flight lead used his radar to lock onto his wingman. This gave him a sure direction to fly to find the runway and safety for the crippled F-86. As the clouds engulfed the tow plane, the F-86 pilot took a fleeting glimpse of the horizon that had allowed him to stay oriented on his own, plunged into the murk, and transitioned to flying formation on the wing of the F-15. With frozen instruments, the big gray fighter plane was his lifeline—his only way of knowing which way was up and which way to the runway.

Minutes passed as the dissimilar formation glided on at the best glide speed for the F-86, the altimeters unwinding toward zero altitude. The F-15, whose engines make a lot of thrust even in idle power, had to extend his speed brake and landing gear to stay with the powerless F-86.

At the OPS desk, we didn't hear anything for a long time. Occasionally we'd hear altitude calls from the F-15 to the F-86: "4,000 . . . 3,000 . . . 2,500 . . ." Just after the "1,500" call we heard what we had been waiting for: "There's the ground. Do you see it? The runway is on your nose for a mile."

There was no response. The battery in the F-86 had died somewhere during the glide, and so the radio had gone dead. Shortly after that call the F-86 peeled out of the formation with the F-15 and set up for a landing pattern.

"Two, he sees runway. Get out of his way," called the flight lead. The landing gear extended from the F-86 Sabre jet, and the pilot made a beautiful dead-stick landing on the crumbling runway.

"He's down—he's landed."

Everyone around the OPS desk began to breathe again. The two F-15s joined up and made a pass over the F-86 on the runway. The F-86 pilot was out of the cockpit standing on the wing and waving his thanks with both arms.

PILOT'S BIOGRAPHY

Rank and branch of service: lieutenant colonel, United States
Air Force, retired

Call sign: Doc

Hometown: McLean, Virginia

Full-time mission: Ohio Columbus

Family: married to Rain Jackson; five children

Church callings: formerly served as bishop, high councilor, and
counselor in bishoprics and branch presidencies; currently
serves as high priest group leader

Current occupation: F-35 test pilot for an aeronautics company

Hobbies: besides Church and family, cars, astronomy, radio-
controlled airplanes

Awards and recognitions: Eagle Scout, distinguished graduate
from United States Air Force Test Pilot School; A1AA Tester
of the Year award, 2001

Dave Nelson flying the F-15

F-4 PHANTOM

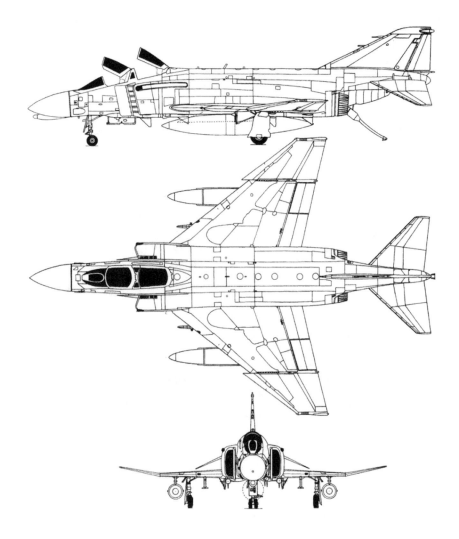

CHAPTER SIX

THUNDERBIRDS TO SOUTH AMERICA

LEONARD MOON

I spent five weeks with the United States Air Force Thunderbirds in South America flying the number eight F-4 Phantom. One of our air shows was at São Jose dos Campos, a small civilian airfield with only a control tower and no hangars between Rio de Janeiro and São Paulo, Brazil. One of the jets required a number one fuel cell change when it began leaking. After the Thunderbirds completed their air show and left for the next stop, I stayed behind with five mechanics to change the fuel cell.

Several days later, we finished the job. The mechanics and tools were loaded into a C-130 cargo aircraft, and they left. I was told to fly to Rio de Janeiro that evening. The next day I would fly to Guatemala, across the Amazon Jungle, with two KC-135 tankers, which would refuel me in the air for the 11-hour flight. It was getting dark and raining very hard. The control tower operator told me the weather was just as bad in Rio. You don't like to hear this when you haven't test-flown a jet that has undergone a major repair, to say nothing of flying to an unfamiliar airfield in bad weather and trying to decipher the Portuguese language when you know only Spanish from having served a Church mission some 16 years earlier.

I told the tower operator to pass my flight plan on to Rio so they would expect me. I had no maps but knew that Rio was northeast of my position and that it would not be a very long flight. I did have some instrument approach and letdown guides to help me find the runway at Rio. My worry was that their navigational aids were not compatible with the newer aids I had in my F-4 Phantom. Before takeoff I prayed and asked for guidance. I felt a little more at ease when both afterburners lit and all instruments indicated the jet would indeed fly.

Once I got close to Rio, I was able to contact the control tower, but the controller informed me that their radar was not functioning on account of the heavy rain. I had really been counting on them to guide me to the airport. The controller said that once I broke out from under the clouds, my visibility would be pretty good, but he cautioned me to adhere to the published minimum altitudes because of the mountainous terrain. He also explained in his broken English that I would need to stay on course because the final approach would bring me just to the left of the huge statue of Christ and to the right of Sugar Loaf Mountain.

This was not very reassuring, because I was trying to use the old radio beacon procedures I had learned years earlier. Those procedures had been abandoned in the United States for the newer tactical navigation system. I flew a couple of circles in the air in the dark as the rain pounded against my canopy. I presented my plan to the Lord and pleaded for his help so that I could "thread the needle," so to speak, between the two obstacles somewhere out there in the darkness. I had been in some tight spots during my two combat tours in Vietnam, but this was also a very high-stress situation. As I centered the navigational needles and pulled the power back to start my descent, I felt a calm come over me that all would be well. I slid down through the thick darkness, hoping to get a glimpse of something other than the black of night. After what seemed an eternity, I broke out of the clouds, and the lights of Rio de Janeiro filled my windscreen.

My prayer had been answered. I took a big deep

breath, a sigh of relief. Off my right wing I was gliding past the magnificent statue of Christ illuminated on a hill. It was at eye level and very close, and the Savior appeared to be standing in midair with his arms out-stretched, as if welcoming me to the great city of Rio de Janeiro. I then saw the runway lights just to my left and made an uneventful landing. Another prayer had been answered, and I spent some time acknowledging that fact.

PILOT'S BIOGRAPHY

Rank and branch of service: colonel, United States Air Force, retired

Hometown: Farmington, Utah

Full-time missions: Spanish-American (Texas and New Mexico); served with his wife in Peru and Bolivia

Family: married to Delores Cunningham; four children; eight grandchildren

Church callings: formerly served as bishop (twice), counselor in two stake presidencies, and high councilor (17 times); currently serves with his wife in the Mexico City Mexico Temple and the Villahermosa Mexico Temple

Current occupation: retired from the Air Force and the admissions office at Brigham Young University

Hobbies: serving full-time missions and spending time with children and grandchildren

Awards and recognitions: Distinguished Flying Cross (two), Air Medal (24), and numerous other recognitions; more than 4,250 hours, including 839 combat hours and 434 combat missions in the F-4 Phantom and F-100 Super Sabre

Captain Moon ready for a combat mission

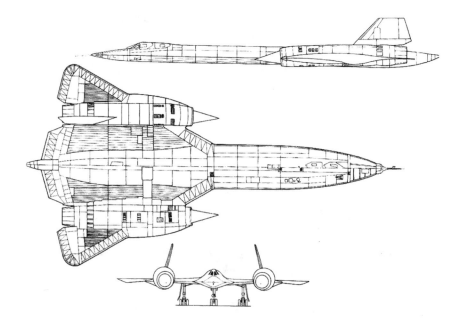

CHAPTER SEVEN

THEY'RE THERE EVERY TIME

GIL BERTELSON

During my 24-year career in the United States Air Force, I was privileged to fly several great airplanes, including the T-38, three different F-111 models (the A, E, and F). Most significant, at least in my mind, was the remarkable and spectacular SR-71. I was one of only 93 Air Force pilots ever qualified to fly it. The SR-71 (SR stood for Strategic Reconnaissance) was designed and built during the days of the Cold War when the two superpowers (the United States and the Soviet Union) were dedicated to gathering intelligence information on each other. The data was then used in the formulation of contingency operations and war plans.

The need to spy on the other guy reached a state of near paranoia at the height of the Cold War. The SR-71 was designed to fill an intelligence collection void that was identified after Gary Powers and his U-2 were shot down on May 1, 1960, while he was flying over the Soviet Union. The shooting down of the U-2 eventually proved very embarrassing for the Eisenhower administration and became the catalyst that caused the cancellation of an extremely important summit conference between the Allied nations (the United States and her friends) and the Warsaw Pact nations (the Soviet Union and her friends).

The shoot-down also made it obvious that the U-2, because of its relatively low flying speed (approximately .85 mach, which is just a little faster than modern airliners) and relatively low flying altitude (approximately 65,000 to 70,000 feet) had become vulnerable to developing Soviet surface-to-air missile (SAM) technology. With famous aircraft designer Kelly Johnson at the lead, a team of engineers at the Lockheed California "Skunk Works" (a term used to describe the Lockheed Advanced Development Program, or ADP) were turned loose to design and build an aircraft that could outrun and outdistance the Soviet Union's new surface-to-air missiles.

After a series of design proposals, the SR-71 ultimately became the product of the Skunk Works efforts. Even by today's standards, it is an amazing looking and performing aircraft. In 1990, nearly 30 years after it was designed, it set four world speed records on a flight from California to Washington, D.C. The coast-to-coast record was 67 minutes, 54 seconds; the Los Angeles-to-Washington, D.C., record was 64 minutes, 20 seconds. The average speed was more than 2,100 miles per hour.

If the SR-71 were still flying today, it could probably break all of those records again. There is nothing in the air or, as far as I know, even in the design stage that can come close to matching, never mind exceeding, its capabilities. I used to get excited to see an SR-71 in the air or even on the ground. Unfortunately, the ground view is all anyone will now see of this remarkable airplane that was, in my opinion, prematurely retired. They now all sit on pedestals in aviation museums throughout the United States and England.

Every time an SR-71 took off, virtually all within hearing or sight distance stopped whatever they were doing and just watched until it was out of sight. It was an almost mesmerizing event. The aircraft always looked to me as if it were traveling at warp speed, even when it was just sitting in the hangar or waiting on the runway for clearance to take off.

The SR-71 has often been described as part aircraft and part spacecraft, and the crewmembers appear to be part pilot and part astronaut. The aircraft was designed to cruise routinely at speeds of over mach 3 and at altitudes above 85,000 feet. To put this in perspective, mach 3 (3 times the speed of sound) and 85,000 feet equate to more than 2,100 miles per hour (over 35 miles per minute) at more than 16 miles above the surface of the earth. If you were flying north in an SR-71 and made a 180-degree, or U, turn to travel south, the two opposing ground tracks would be 175 miles apart.

When we flew missions over the Baltic Sea and certain parts of Europe, we had to fly at mach 2.8 because at mach 3 our velocity would force us over territory that, for political reasons, we were supposed to avoid. For many years, the actual top speed and altitude of the aircraft were classified. Only after the airplane's retirement in 1997 were the official capabilities made available to the general public. And what amazing figures they are—the top speed is listed as mach 3.3 or above, while the maximum altitude is listed as 90,000 feet or above. The "or above" statements are there because various factors, such as the outside air temperature at high altitude, have a significant effect on the aircraft's performance.

Because of the altitudes we attained on every

mission, we were required to wear full pressure, or space, suits just like those worn by NASA astronauts in the space shuttle. At our normal cruising altitudes we were above 98 percent of the earth's atmosphere. In that environment, if we were to have a cockpit pressurization failure, we would have faced certain and instantaneous death if we didn't have the backup protection of the pressure suit. The space suit was bulky and heavy (about 40 pounds), but it was an absolute necessity for safety in the hostile environment where we routinely flew.

Even though there was virtually no atmosphere at our cruising altitudes, we were flying so fast through what little remained that skin friction (like rubbing your hands together) between the surfaces of the aircraft and the tiny bit of remaining atmosphere would generate temperatures on the airplane that ranged between 600 and 1500 degrees Fahrenheit.

One of my most memorable SR-71 flights occurred on one of numerous missions I flew over the Barents Sea, which is just off the northern coast of Finland and Russia in the vicinity of Murmansk. From our departure base at RAF Mildenhall in England, we'd fly northward over the Northern Atlantic Sea and along the coast of Norway. On a clear day, the view of the Norwegian fjords from 85,000 to 90,000 feet is one of the most spectacular sights I've ever seen. We were actually high enough that we could distinctly see the curvature of the earth. At the northernmost end of Norway, we'd turn east, where we would shortly enter the area of the Barents Sea. We were there primarily to gather imagery (radar or photographic) of the Soviet Union's northern submarine fleet.

In a very early scene in the movie *The Hunt for Red October,* actor Sean Connery (playing the role of a Soviet submarine commander) is shown on the conning tower of the *Red October* as it slips through the "Polijarny Inlet" on its maiden voyage, en route to the open waters of the Atlantic Ocean. This was the general area where we routinely flew to gather information required by various United States intelligence agencies. The United States and our allies needed to know how many Soviet ballistic missile submarines were still in port so they could determine how many of them were out to sea and might pose a potential missile threat to the United States or its allies. The United States Navy was responsible for finding and tracking all the missile submarines that were, in fact, out to sea.

This particular January day happened to be one of those when the outside air temperature had a significant effect on the performance of the airplane. The air is typically very cold (normally about minus 56 degrees centigrade) at the altitudes where we usually flew. But on this day it was exceptionally cold—about 30 degrees centigrade colder than normal, or minus 85 degrees centigrade.

The airplane was performing perfectly. I had the throttles positioned at the absolute minimum afterburner setting, and yet I was having a hard time keeping the speed down to mach 3, which was the speed the mission had been planned for.

As we departed our base in England, I noticed (through a small periscope-type piece of equipment that provided me a very limited view behind the airplane) that we were leaving a contrail as we climbed through 13,000 feet. It was normal to leave a trail like this at some time on every mission, but it usually didn't start until we passed through 25,000 to 30,000 feet going up. And we would usually stop leaving the contrail somewhere around 40,000 to 45,000 feet during the climb out.

Contrails are a normal happening when engine exhaust heat mixes with cold, humid air. From the pilot's perspective, however, they're not a welcome sight when flying in the vicinity of an avowed adversary, as I was at this particular time. I'd never heard of contrails forming behind an aircraft once it got above 45,000 to 50,000 feet.

Well, this day was not like other days. As I said, we started leaving the telltale contrail passing through 13,000 feet as we left England, and we didn't once stop leaving the contrail until descending through 13,000 feet over England, four and a half hours and three air-to-air refuelings later, as we prepared to land.

As we flew over the Barents Sea on this cold, crisp, and very clear day in January, we were announcing, by our bright and distinct contrail, our exact location and direction to the entire Soviet air force and anyone else who happened to look up at the right time. I had only recently visited with a former Soviet MiG-25 pilot who had announced to me that the dream of every MiG-25 pilot was to shoot down an SR-71. In spite of his comment and the circumstances of the day, I knew there was little to be concerned about as long as the aircraft continued to perform as it presently was.

We made a pass along the northern Soviet coast, heading from west to east. We then turned north toward the Arctic Circle. A short time later, we made one of those 175-mile-radius U turns. The radius was actually a little larger than 175 miles that day, however, because of how cold the air was in comparison to what we had been briefed by the weatherman. After completing the turn, our next objective was to merely head back toward the Soviet border and, at the last minute, make a 90-degree right turn to again parallel the coastline and head west. We were to continue the westerly heading until we were once again off Norway. Then it would only be a matter of slowing down and descending for a final in-flight refueling before making the final supersonic leg to our home base in England.

Everything was going normally, just as it always had on past Barents Sea missions, until we were

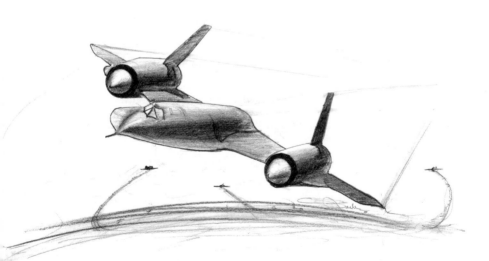

approaching the right turn toward Norway. The first unusual thing I noticed was that the contrails we had created 45 minutes ago were still there. In fact, we flew right through portions of the old trails. As I completed the right turn toward the west, I looked out the left side of the airplane to discover 12 to 15 contrails coming from the Soviet coastline and streaking up towards us.

There was no real cause for alarm because of our speed and altitude. No other airplane anywhere in the world could reach us or catch us. And as long as those intercepting contrails were abeam or behind our position, as they were, there was no threat from any air-to-air missiles they might be carrying.

Yet a little hint of concern passed through my mind because of the big, long, white streak trailing our airplane, which pointed directly to our position in the sky. If the interceptors could see my contrail as well as I could see theirs, there wouldn't be much doubt in their minds about where we were. And I remembered the statement of the Soviet pilot who had defected to the United States several years before: "It's the dream of every MiG–25 pilot to shoot down an SR-71."

When we got safely back to England, we began the process of debriefing the mission, which always consisted of several steps. First, we spent time with the maintenance folks to tell them about any problems we might have had with the airplane. They wanted to get an early start on any needed repairs. Then the weatherman came in to find out how closely he had forecast the weather for our flight that day. (Needless to say, we had some fun with his high altitude temperature predictions.) Last, the intelligence folks sat down to talk to us. After we discussed mission objectives and weather phenomena that might have affected the photo or radar images we were trying to gather, I told them about the "excitement" of the intercepting contrails. I expected a response like "Wow," or "Tell us that again. Is that what really happened?"

Instead, I was told in a very matter-of-fact tone of voice: "So what? They're there every time you fly over the Barents."

Well, I thought, *thanks for sharing that with us ahead of time. It might have been useful information to pass along in the premission briefing.*

We continued to fly over the Barents Sea, and I suppose the Soviets continued to practice their intercepts against us. We never did identify any actual hostile intent on their part. As I've reflected on that particular day and the events that took place, I learned an important gospel lesson because of my participation in that particular military operation:

Satan's influence is so subtle that at times it's almost invisible. All through our lives temptations follow us, and we may not even recognize them. Sometimes they may seem like little things, little distractions, that do not amount to much.

On other occasions, the Lord may open our eyes and help us see with great clarity the source of these "little" temptations—they come from the adversary himself, who is determined to take us off course and destroy us. In fact, it is his intent to "shoot down" a child of God whenever and however he can. The adversary is constantly on the prowl, even though at times we may not see or recognize him. He's there, every time.

We need to stay above the temptations and stay on the course our Father in Heaven has outlined. Although the temptations will follow us, if we stay focused on our goals and our final destination, they will never get close enough to destroy us.

PILOT'S BIOGRAPHY

Rank and branch of service: lieutenant colonel, United States
Air Force, retired

Hometown: Provo, Utah

Full-time mission: California Mission

Family: married to Loye Draayer; four daughters; 10
grandchildren

Church callings: formerly served as bishop (twice), counselor
in a stake presidency, and high councilor; currently serves
as Gospel Doctrine teacher in his ward

Current occupation: retired as director of the Executive MBA
program at the BYU Marriott School of Management;
serves as a tour guide at Hill Air Force Base Aerospace
Museum and as president-elect of the Salt Lake chapter
of the BYU Management Society

Hobbies: family, golf, skiing, fishing, traveling

Awards and recognitions: Defense Meritorious Service Medal,
Air Medal (three), Meritorious Service Medal (three), Air
Force Commendation Medal (four), Combat Readiness
Medal (two), National Defense Service Medal

Gil Bertelson (left) and Frank Stampf with SR-71

CHAPTER EIGHT

IF YE ARE PREPARED YE SHALL NOT FEAR

RICK SEARFOSS

April 17, 1998, was launch day of my third space mission and the first I would command. I'd prepared my entire professional life for this moment, including many thousands of hours flying and testing high-performance aircraft, eight years in the astronaut corps, two previous space flights, and more than a year guiding my crew of seven during intense mission-specific training. I would lead the flight crew of the most ambitious and complex science research human space mission ever undertaken to that point, the STS-90 Neurolab flight on the space shuttle *Columbia*. Together we would spend two and a half weeks in orbit as we studied the workings of the brain and nervous system in the incredible environment of weightlessness. Preparation was paramount.

Our group of astronauts represented phenomenal

technical talent: three doctors, a veterinarian, an engineer, and another military test pilot like me. Yet five of them were rookies, first-time space flyers, and I'd been given the charge to really prepare them for any eventuality. It had been a great year, working as hard as any of us ever had, leaving no stone unturned in the preparation, with me constantly teaching and relating to the crew just what real space flight would be like. I had pushed the rookies hard, and they had responded even more magnificently than I'd expected. After thousands of hours of practice, including too many simulator runs to keep track of, we could virtually read each other's minds. We knew we could handle the challenge of operating the most complex aerospace vehicle ever built. I felt we had prepared as well as any space crew ever had.

It is indeed true that "if ye are prepared ye shall not fear" (D&C 38:30). But complete preparation goes beyond study and hard work. Just a week previously I'd received a blessing at the hands of my stake leaders. This blessing offered great confidence-building promises about the upcoming launch and my role as the first Latter-day Saint commander of a space mission. It played a crucial part in completing my personal preparation. Yet when I awoke some seven hours before the launch, there still remained one last crew preparation activity. I had scheduled a private meeting, flight crew only, one-half hour prior to the time when we would don our orange spacesuits. As we gathered I expressed how pleased I was with our preparation, how confident I was that everyone would perform superbly, and how grateful I was to be on the same team with them. I shared my testimony that going into space would be a humbling and overpowering, even spiritual, experience and that our preparations alone would not totally suffice for the challenge ahead. With their agreement, I offered a prayer that our Father in Heaven would bless our efforts, protect *Columbia,* and see us home again safely to our families. Finally our preparations were complete. We could suit up and head to the launch pad!

An hour later we boarded the astrovan for the trip to the launch pad. We were excited, confident, and joking. During that 10-minute drive, the mood grew more reflective, even reverent, until we stopped at the base of the pad right beneath the hulking stack of a fully fueled space shuttle. Pausing momentarily, we drank in the overwhelming view of a behemoth that seemed eager to spring off into the heavens. After strap-in and an uneventful countdown, six seconds prior to launch

Columbia came alive as her three main engines powered up. At liftoff we felt an incredibly powerful shove as more than six million pounds of thrust from the ignition of the solid rocket boosters kicked in to send us on our way.

STS–90 leaves the launch pad, April 17, 1998

After my radio call of "Roll program, Houston," I had a momentary glimpse of the thousands of people stationed along the causeway to view the launch—folks who would still be fighting the traffic after we'd already circled the planet. The ascent was eight and a half minutes of sheer exhilaration mixed, for me and the copilot, with second-by-second attention to all the system performance details we'd worked so hard to master. Then, from being pressed against the seat and weighing nearly 600 pounds each from the acceleration, at main engine cutoff we made the startling instant transition to the wondrous floating freedom of weightlessness. We enjoyed that delicious floating sensation and the most glorious and awe-inspiring views of planet Earth for 16 days while working as hard as we ever had in our lives to meet the mission goals, all the while further cementing the bonds of fellowship with each other that had grown during training. Gazing down at the peaceful view of our home planet below, I was often struck with the contrast that view was to the very real, trying, and tragic circumstances in so many corners of the world—the Middle East and portions of Africa, in particular.

As the mission wound down and we completed the scientific objectives, it was time for the mildly bittersweet feeling of leaving space behind. It's such a fantastic experience that part of you never wants it to end, yet at the same time you long to reunite with family members, look into their eyes, and share the infinite wonders you've seen. The night before reentry I took a few minutes to review some of my favorite inspirational scriptures I had copied into my crew note-book, pondered the work ahead of me the next day to get my crew and America's spaceship home safely, and asked the Lord's help with that task. My first mission commander had said to me, "It's different being the commander because it will always be in your mind that you have the ultimate responsibility to finish the mission safely with your landing." He was right—I had carried that burden the whole mission. Yet I also had great confidence from years of hard work and training, the support and prayers of friends and family, and my own reliance on Heavenly Father.

On our last of 256 orbits we turned around to make our retrograde burn somewhere over the Indian Ocean, slowing by only a few hundred miles per hour our incredible 17,600-mph orbital velocity. But it was sufficient to begin the descent into the waiting atmosphere below, which decelerated us all the way to our landing speed of about 230 mph, generating blast-furnace type heat in the process. In one hour *Columbia* went from an orbiting spacecraft hurtling through the blackness of space to being parked on a runway with lush green grass and palm trees all around, swaying in the Florida spring breeze. And what a stupendous hour—the uniquely colored pinkish-orange glow of the hot plasma gases flowing past the window, the screaming rush as we ripped across the southwestern United States at 20 times the speed of sound only 40 miles up, and rolling out on high final approach at 300 knots to see that beautiful runway fall perfectly into place under the symbols on my heads-up display.

Finally, much as I'd done more than a thousand times in the shuttle trainer aircraft—but this time for real—I called upon my piloting skills to make a safe, controlled touchdown back on planet Earth.

After rolling to a stop, calling "Houston, Columbia, wheel stop," and quietly saying a private prayer of

Columbia lands in Florida

thanks, it was high fives all around the flight deck. Home safe and sound, after more than six million miles. Thirty minutes later, crawling through the hatch, I paused and turned for a view of the flight deck where I'd spent more time than any other previous astronaut with my two very long missions on *Columbia*. Later, the thought came that sometime in the future, when this grand lady of the fleet, the first space shuttle, was retired to the Smithsonian, I'd have a chance to show her to my grandkids. I smiled as I contemplated saying, "Look, kids, here's where Grandpa used to work." Such was not to be, however, for with her gallant crew just a few flights later, *Columbia* was lost in the enduring human quest for knowledge, understanding, and exploration.

The Neurolab mission was incredibly productive, exceeding by far every mission goal. And *Columbia* flew with fewer in-flight anomalies than it ever had in 25 flights. Even when a critical piece of life support equipment did malfunction in an unanticipated way never seen before in ground testing, by working with mission control we were able to repair it in space. Over and over again as we circled the Earth, the crew and I performed beyond our natural abilities. Was all this the fruit of preparation and dedication? Yes, but not exclusively preparation and dedication as the world sees it. I'm firmly convinced that the willingness and desire of all seven of us, along with our families, friends, and colleagues, to exercise faith, acknowledge the Lord's hand, and entreat his blessing in a worthy endeavor made the difference.

PILOT'S BIOGRAPHY

Rank and branch of service: colonel, United States Air Force, retired

Call sign: Pops

Hometown: Portsmouth, New Hampshire

Family: married to Julie McGuire Searfoss; three children

Church callings: currently serves as high priest group instructor

Current occupation: professional speaker (www.astronaut-speaker.com), consultant, and test pilot for an aerospace company

Awards and recognitions: United States Air Force Meritorious Service Medal, NASA Exceptional Service Medal, NASA Outstanding Leadership Medal, Air Force Distinguished Flying Cross, Legion of Merit, Defense Superior Service Medal, and others

Rick Searfoss

F-4 PHANTOM

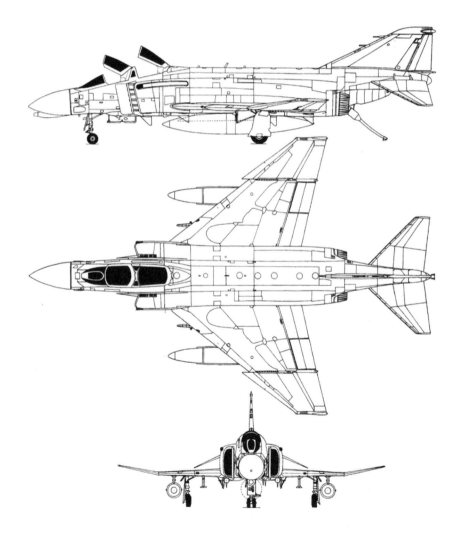

CHAPTER NINE

ALMOST SHOT DOWN

LEONARD MOON

After spending 1969 in Vietnam flying 227 combat missions in the F-100 Super Sabre, I found myself in May 1971 heading for another one-year tour in Thailand flying the F-4 Phantom. That year, like the first, I had many close calls, but I had made it to within a couple of days before I was to go home again. The policy was that when we got within a week of going home, we no longer had to fly missions into North Vietnam. Missions during that last week were to the Saigon area, where the chance of getting shot down was much less than up north.

I had only two more missions to fly. That day's mission was to be the flight leader of a two-ship flight to South Vietnam. My ordnance load was nine large canisters of napalm, and my wingman carried nine 500-pound high-drag bombs. As the sun was sinking toward the western horizon, we took off, heading southeast from Korat Royal Thai Air Base. Our target area would be about an hour and a half away. At about the halfway point, the C-130 command post called to divert us to help some marines who were under intense fire near the DMZ—the demilitarized zone on the border between North and South Vietnam. We were the only jets airborne and could get there the quickest. They told us to turn northeast for an hour's flight to the target area. They said they would send an in-flight refueling tanker in our direction, because we would need to be refueled before getting to the target. Then we were told that the target was a small, walled-in village in the middle of the jungle. The North Vietnamese regular army was trying to breach the walls of the city with ladders, and the United States Marines were trying to hold them off. It sounded like a Book of Mormon battle.

This was all I needed two days before going home. I had time to think about my situation and to discuss with my Heavenly Father how much I needed his guidance and protection on this most dangerous mission. As we flew northeast my mind returned to when I left home almost a year earlier. I left a beautiful pregnant wife, two little boys, and only the foundation completed on our new home. Since then, my wife had finished our home and given birth to our first daughter. I told the Lord of my need to return home. Then my thoughts turned to my cousin Jay C. Hess, who was a prisoner of war (POW) somewhere in North Vietnam. He had been there more than four years, and I hoped that I would not meet the same fate that he had.

After we refueled and neared the target area, I contacted the marines, who asked me to have my wingman drop his bombs a short distance from the village in the jungle area, which he did. This somewhat slowed down the advance of the enemy. The marine commander asked that I drop the napalm, all nine canisters, one right after the other, right on top of the wall surrounding the village. From several miles out and at an altitude where I could line up with the wall of the village, I started my descent to tree-top level. I pushed the power up and set up my bombing switches. I descended to about 50 feet above the trees and noted the indicated air speed was 600 miles per hour. I figured that at this speed and at a low altitude the enemy gunners would not see me until I was right on top of them. As I flew along the wall dropping the canisters, I could see the enemy running from the wall and saw tracers flying past my canopy.

As I pulled off the target the marine commander radioed that the napalm run was perfect and thanked us for our efforts. As I climbed away from the target, I noticed that there were no warning lights on my instruments, so I figured that I had not been hit by enemy fire. I felt a rush come over me, feeling that I had received the protection I had asked for. As my wingman joined on my right wing, he radioed me that I had a jagged hole one foot in diameter in the top portion of my right wing from enemy ground fire. It was near the engine nacelle and right over the wing fuel tank. He could not see any fuel leaking, and I confirmed, by the fuel gauges, that I was not losing fuel. It was a long journey back to our air base, with a lot of pleading to the Lord to help me get back.

After what seemed like an eternity, we arrived at our air base, and I made an emergency landing. Later I found out that I had been hit with a 37-millimeter exploding shell that penetrated the bottom of the wing but did not explode until it exited the top of the wing. If it had hit even an inch forward of where it hit, it would have penetrated the hot air duct, which would have burned through the insulation surrounding the wing fuel tank, which could have burned into the wing fuel tank. If it had hit an inch farther back, it would have penetrated the wing fuel cell, which was full of fuel at the time. Either way the wing could have been blown off. The two-inch area between the fuel cell and the hot air duct was filled with insulation, so nothing critical was hit. If I had been a millisecond faster or slower, the outcome could have been much more serious.

When I learned from my wingman that I had been hit, I almost felt that my previous prayer had not been answered. Once I landed and found out how very fortunate I really was, I realized that my prayer had been answered, and I again thanked the Lord. The next day

I flew my last mission without incident, and the following day I was on the "Freedom Bird," heading home to my family. A year later I was in charge of the huge welcome home celebration at the Davis County Court House in Farmington, Utah, for my POW cousin, Jay C. Hess.

PILOT'S BIOGRAPHY

Rank and branch of service: colonel, United States Air Force, retired

Hometown: Farmington, Utah

Full-time missions: Spanish-American (Texas and New Mexico); served with his wife in Peru and Bolivia

Family: married to Delores Cunningham; four children; eight grandchildren

Church callings: formerly served as bishop (twice), counselor in two stake presidencies, and high councilor (17 times); currently serves with his wife in the Mexico City Mexico Temple and the Villahermosa Mexico Temple

Current occupation: retired from the Air Force and the admissions office at Brigham Young University

Hobbies: serving full-time missions and spending time with children and grandchildren

Awards and recognitions: Distinguished Flying Cross (two), Air Medal (24), and numerous other recognitions; more than 4,250 hours, including 839 combat hours and 434 combat missions in the F-4 Phantom and F-100 Super Sabre

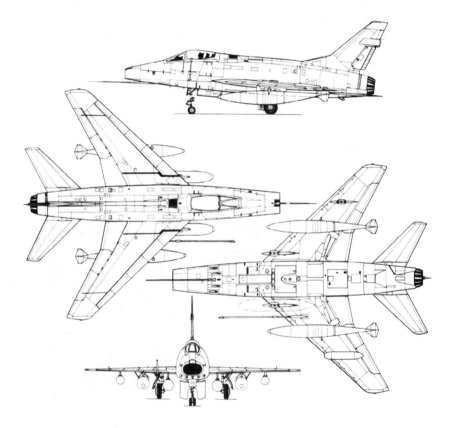

CHAPTER TEN

A TORNADO IN THE COCKPIT

THALES A. "TAD" DERRICK

A crystal-clear dawn was breaking during the summer of 1960 as I parked my white 1956 Buick Century hardtop in the parking lot behind the 4514th Combat Crew Training Squadron (CCTS) at Luke AFB, Arizona. Several other cars were already there—some students' cars and some instructors' cars. I recognized the cars belonging to Paladin and Jigger, the call signs of two instructors who were also assigned to early-morning missions. My call sign was Meteor. The name was adapted from the famous Salt Flats racing car of the 1950s—*The Mormon Meteor.* (Ab Jenkins, who drove the *Meteor,* was my hero as I grew up in Salt Lake City, Utah, and he was also the mayor of Salt Lake City.)

The squadron briefing room was already abuzz with conversations when I entered. Paladin and Jigger had the first and second takeoff times. Each instructor would lead three students on air-to-ground gunnery missions. Meteor flight had the third takeoff time. Paladin and Jigger had their students in separate briefing cubicles and were starting their briefings. I greeted my three students, and together we checked the weather for the flight. It was going to remain clear, and the wind was calm. It was an ideal morning for flying. My students and I picked up our flight briefing cards and settled into an otherwise empty briefing cubicle that held a small rectangular table, four chairs, and a briefing blackboard with special sliding briefing boards for different kinds of missions.

The students assigned to the 4514th CCTS had graduated recently from United States Air Force (USAF) pilot training, received their wings, and had about 250 hours of flight time, mostly in jet trainers. They were students from the very top of their class. Typically, students chose their assignments out of pilot training based upon class standing. Most often, the top students chose to become fighter pilots. They were highly motivated. They had come, by choice, to Luke AFB to be checked out in the F-100C Super Sabre jet fighter and for the first time learn to use an aircraft as a weapon. These students were excellent young pilots and instructing them was a privilege. The three students flying with me on this mission were solid, and I looked forward to an excellent flight.

My mission today would be air-to-ground gunnery, like the Paladin and Jigger flights. All the students had completed transition and formation flying previously in the F-100C. The flight briefing followed a familiar format: preflight, engine start, radio check-in, taxi, gun and rocket arming at the end of the runway, two-ship formation takeoffs with me as flight leader (number one) and my wingman (number two) rolling first and then number three with his wingman (number four) rolling 15 seconds behind us. After takeoff and accelerating to 300 knots, flight leader and number two would come out of afterburner and gradually accelerate to 350 knots while numbers three and four completed a straight ahead join-up. Meteor flight would then proceed as a flight of four fighters to Range 1 on the Gila Bend Gunnery Range, about 50 miles south of Luke AFB. The flight would split up over the range, and each pilot would make individual runs. The gunnery events would consist of four skip bomb passes from an altitude of 50 feet above the ground, four rocket passes using a dive angle of 30, four dive bomb passes using a dive angle of 45, and finally 20mm cannon strafing passes at a dive angle of 10. All deliveries would be made at 400 knots indicated airspeed. The flight would then rejoin into a flight-of-four formation, depart the range complex, and return to Luke for landing. The flight would use a standard fighter approach with the four aircraft in echelon formation on initial and at 300 knots. The lead aircraft would "break left" over the end of the runway with each student following at four-second intervals. Final approach speed would be 180 knots (the F-100C did not have wing flaps, so approach speed was high). Students were briefed to start their power reduction about 1,000 feet from touchdown so as to land no farther than 1,000 feet down the 10,000-foot runway. Nose wheel steering was to be engaged immediately and the drag chute deployed to aid in braking. Drag chutes were to be dropped after turning off the end of the runway, guns de-armed, any unused rockets made safe, and then the Meteor flight would taxi to the parking area on the ramp. All pilots would be picked up by the squadron van and returned to the squadron for debriefing. (Note: 1 knot equals 1.15 miles per hour, so 180 knots equals 207 mph, 200 knots equals 230 mph, 300 knots equals 345 mph, 400 knots equals 460 mph, etc.)

The briefing was completed on schedule, and the pilots proceeded to the equipment room to pick up their flight helmets, g-suits, and parachutes. The banter was lighthearted on the way to the aircraft, and a couple of "soft drink" bets were made by the students about who would get the best gunnery scores.

With each aircraft's engine running and at the prescribed time, I called for the radio check-in on squadron frequency: "Meteor flight—check." The students responded crisply, "Two," "Three," "Four."

"Roger, Meteors; go channel two"—and again the crisp reply, "Two," "Three," "Four."

When on channel two, I called, "Meteor flight—check."

"Two," "Three," "Four."

"Roger; Luke Tower, four Meteors for taxi."

"Roger, Meteor; taxi runway two-one left."

"Roger; two-one left."

The flight then taxied to the arming area adjacent to runway two-one left. After arming, the flight switched to takeoff frequency and was cleared into position for engine run-up. The fighters lined up with my aircraft just right of centerline and my wingman, number two, with just wingtip clearance to my right. Number three lined up with the nose of his aircraft in the space between lead and number two with number four to his left. Wheel brakes were held tightly while engines were run up to full nonafterburner power and the engine performance instruments checked for normal operation. Number four then nodded to number three when he was satisfied with his aircraft, number three nodded to number two, and number two nodded to lead. At this point, we were a go.

I reduced my power slightly to give number two some advantage in maintaining position, leaned my head back against the seat headrest, and then dropped it forward as the signal for number two to release his brakes. A second nod signaled to light the afterburner. I checked number two for a good burner light, and we accelerated rapidly down the runway. Number two held perfect formation during the takeoff roll. As I looked over at number two to signal I was beginning nose wheel liftoff, I was startled to see his clamshell canopy sliding back and starting to open!

Before I could warn him, we were airborne and his canopy was still opening. We were now approaching 200 knots. The canopy continued to open to a point about halfway between full open and closed, and there it stopped, like a giant mouth scooping in 200-knot tornado force wind! (An open canopy was supposed to shear off above 50 knots.) We now were way too far down the runway to attempt a landing. Number two began to fall out of formation and settle back toward the ground. I radioed, "Meteor Two, pull up, pull up!"

He stopped his descent as we crossed the end of the runway and just held level at about 50 feet above the ground. He barely missed some tall trees about a half mile off the end of the runway, and by then I was screaming for him to pull up. I came out of afterburner so as to hold position near the student's aircraft. The student too moved his throttle out of the afterburner range.

I could see the student in the cockpit, and it was obvious he was taking a beating from the violent wind blast. Finally, he seemed to hear and see me. I was about 20 feet above him and about 50 feet off to his left side. I called, "Gear up!"

He responded by retracting his landing gear. (I later learned that when the canopy first came open, the wind blast blew dirt and dust off the cockpit floor into his eyes, blinding him temporarily.) I instructed him to turn his radio volume up full blast, and we then were able to communicate a bit easier.

I wished I could slow down, but I didn't know what the flying characteristics would be below 200 knots. I held what we had and started a slow turn over an unpopulated area back toward the base. I had the

student take the lead position of the flight so he would not have to look to the side. This gave him better vision because the basic windscreen shielded his eyes somewhat. His helmet visor and oxygen mask also protected his face.

I told the other two members of my flight, Meteor numbers three and four, to burn off fuel in the transition area as two singles and then return to base for landing. Students were not allowed to fly formation without an instructor and were not allowed to go to the gunnery range without an instructor, for obvious reasons.

The mobile control unit at the end of the runway was a frenzy of activity. It was manned by F-100 pilots prepared to give assistance in an emergency. (Mobile control, rather than the control tower, directed emergency operations.) We discussed options: First, it was agreed that the student pilot should not touch "anything" because he was still flying and had control. Second, no one had ever heard of this happening. It was not covered in the flight manual. Third, the aircraft manufacturer, North American Rockwell, would be called on the command-post hot line for recommendations. Fourth, we discussed trying to close the canopy using the normal electrical switch. Fifth, we talked about trying to jettison the canopy by pulling the explosive jettison handle. Sixth, we considered having the student eject. Seventh, we deliberated attempting a landing with the canopy open. The call to North American Rockwell test pilots came up with the same options we had discussed already. This was "a first," and North American Rockwell was anxious to know what we decided and what the outcome was.

When no clear procedure or directive is in place, the pilot in command is given the authority to "call the shot." Since I was on the scene and in command of the flight, the final decision would be between me and the student pilot. I knew the student would rely heavily upon my judgment. I was just a first lieutenant, so making such a critical decision weighed heavily upon my mind.

It was a time for a hurried prayer. I prayed, *Heavenly Father, I need Thy counsel quickly. My student's life may well be at risk with the decision I make. Please help me think clearly and make the decision that will save him.*

I felt peace. As we approached the airfield, an F-100 pilot in mobile control called on the radio, "Meteor, what are your intentions?"

I spoke my mind calmly. "Mobile, the electrical switch option doesn't appeal to me because the canopy might not close and could even open further if the switch is shorted. It might then rip off and perhaps destroy the vertical fin and rudder. The jettison option doesn't offer a guarantee of a clean separation, either, because all jettison tests were done from a closed canopy position. The canopy could 'dish' into the cockpit and perhaps hit the student in the head. Having the student eject is not a positive option, either. If the canopy stayed where it is now during the ejection, the canopy bow would probably break the student's legs [read, 'kill the pilot']. I recommend that we land the airplane. I will fly the student's wing during the approach and coach him on airspeed and altitude. I'll hand him off to mobile control when we are approaching touchdown."

The student had of course heard all the chatter on the radio, and I asked him, "Meteor Two, are you ready to attempt the landing option?"

He said simply, "Roger, Meteor lead."

Mobile control concurred. "Roger, Meteor."

I asked the control tower to divert all other landing traffic to Williams AFB on the other side of the Phoenix valley. The Paladin and Jigger flights, along with others, would get a little extra flying time. The tower agreed, so we had the airspace to ourselves.

While still at about 3,000 feet of altitude, I had the student run through a landing sequence by lowering the speed brake and landing gear and gradually slowing the aircraft to 190 knots. I was confident that even if he landed "hot" (at a higher than normal speed), he could stop with the aid of the drag chute or even by using the arresting cable barrier at the far end of the runway. The open canopy would also help slow the aircraft. We found that the aircraft was still quite stable at 190 knots.

I then instructed the student to set up for a long, straight-in approach and to take his time. As he started a turn toward the final approach, he suddenly rolled wings level and indicated he wanted to try again. He then made a huge circle back to the final approach. I didn't question the maneuver because I couldn't guess what he was facing in terms of control issues in a turn.

When lined up on the final approach, I requested full radio silence, so I would have a clear channel to coach the approach. I then said, "Meteor Two, when you are ready, lower the speed brake and put the gear down."

In a few seconds, he lowered his speed brake, followed by the landing gear. I lowered mine. I then moved into a close formation position on his right wing, so I would know exactly what his airspeed was at all times. I instructed, "Meteor Two, start your descent now. Continue to hold 200 knots."

The student started a picture-perfect descent and held his airspeed on the money. About one-half mile from the end of the runway we were "in the groove," and I said, "Meteor Two, slow to 190 knots."

We slowed smoothly. As we crossed over the end of the overrun, I said, "Meteor Two, you've got it made."

"Mobile, you've got him."

Then I applied full power, maneuvered to my right, and commenced a go-around. Mobile control talked Meteor Two through the touchdown, drag-chute deployment, braking, speed brake retraction, and finally engine shutdown. He stopped well short of the "barrier."

I flew around for a few minutes while the de-arming crew disarmed the guns and made the rockets safe and the maintenance crew towed the airplane off of the runway.

When the runway reopened, I landed and went through the normal after-landing drill. Meteor Two had been checked by the flight surgeon, and other than scratches, minor cuts and abrasions from shoulder harness and parachute, he was pronounced just fine. Meteor Two said he felt like he had played both ways for a full football game. There was the normal round of handshaking and backslapping in the squadron. The squadron commander and the wing commander greeted us and commended us for some good flying.

When things quieted down, I asked Meteor Two why he rolled out of the first turn to final approach. He said he felt he was losing rudder control. This made perfect sense. The partially open canopy was probably blocking the rudder somewhat even in straight and level flight. He made a very good decision.

After I debriefed the students and had a moment to myself, I went out to the parking lot and sat on the red-and-white rolled leather seat of my Buick Century and bowed my head in a prayer of gratitude: *Heavenly Father, I thank Thee for the decision Thou guided me to make this morning. I'm thankful my student and I were able to land safely. I thank Thee, too, for the opportunity to fly and to fly fighters. Please look after all of us so engaged.*

PILOT'S BIOGRAPHY

Rank and branch of service: lieutenant colonel, United States
Air Force, retired

Call sign: Meteor

Hometowns: Salt Lake City and St. George, Utah (since 1974)

Family: married to Willa Nita Brooks; five children; 22 grandchildren

Church callings: formerly served as bishop, stake president,
and president of Pennsylvania Pittsburgh Mission, 1992–
95; currently serves as Gospel Doctrine teacher

Current occupation: retired

Hobbies: flying his own airplane, growing fruit trees and gar-
dening, spending time with grandchildren

Awards and recognitions: Distinguished Flying Cross, Air Medal
(five), Meritorious Service (three), among others

*Tad Derrick with an F-100C fighter when he was named Instructor of the
Month at Luke Air Force Base, Arizona, 1960*

O-1 BIRD DOG

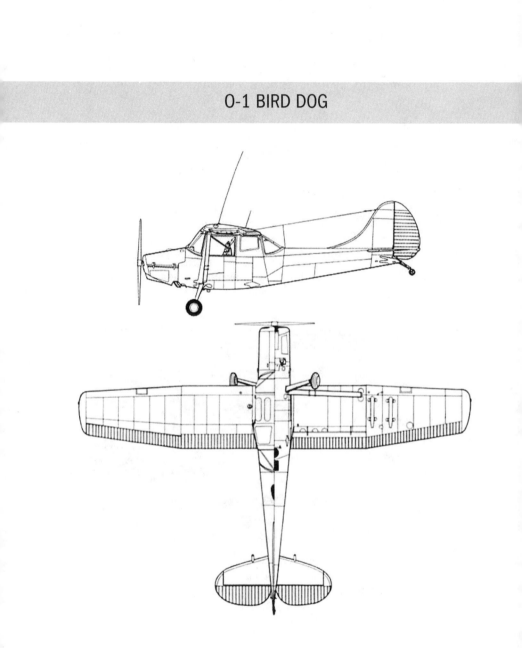

CHAPTER ELEVEN

DISTINGUISHED FLYING CROSS

OSCAR R. "RON" ADAMS

The day started like most days lately—clear, hot, and humid. I had been assigned to a pretty routine mission, flying as a forward air controller in a O-1 Bird Dog. The mission was a strike on a supposed Viet Cong base camp near Quan Loi, near the Cambodian border. Upon arriving at the coordinates of the camp and before the flight of fighters arrived, I looked the area over. It seemed a pretty peaceful place. There was a lot of triple canopy jungle with a number of open areas. These open areas were covered with elephant grass about three to five feet high. I picked out the area of the suspected camp near a stream. Most of these camps were underground and hard to find until we could drop bombs and open them up.

The fighters checked in, Dice flight out of Bien Hoa. I gave them my position and asked them for the type of ordnance (bombs, rockets, etc.) they were carrying. Dice 01 reported they were carrying 500-pound bombs. I briefed them on the area: no friendlies around, the direction to attack from, and—in case of trouble and they had to eject—where to head for a safe area. I rolled in and fired one of my smoke rockets to mark the target and then directed Dice 01 where to drop his bomb relative to my mark. I cleared him in to drop, turned to follow him to see where he dropped, and then directed Dice 02 to drop his bomb, corrected from lead's bomb.

We did this a couple of times, trying to cover the area and open up any bunkers that might be down in the trees. On the third pass, lead reported that he thought he was receiving ground fire from the area. I had not yet seen any. Dice 02 came in for his third drop and pulled off the target. As I rolled around to pick up Dice 01, he came on the radio declaring an emergency—Dice 02 had just ejected from his plane.

As I turned my plane around to locate Dice 02, I found him above and behind me. His chute had just opened, and he was in a slow descent. I immediately called on the emergency frequency to put out the word that we had a downed pilot and to alert air rescue. I flew toward the descending pilot and watched him land in one of the large, open triangle-shaped areas near the tree line.

After he was on the ground, I contacted him on his emergency radio and told him to stay where he was. He said he was okay and in about five feet of elephant grass.

I returned to the radios. Dice 01 said he could fly for about five more minutes and then he was "bingo fuel," meaning his fuel was low and he needed to return to base. I called my command post and asked for more air cover. They said they were diverting a flight of F-4s to my location and were ordering up another flight.

Just about that time, I could see emerging from the opposite tree line a large number of enemy soldiers looking for the downed airman. I began orbiting over an area away from the downed airman and the approaching troops, hoping to make them believe that I was over the downed airman, in an attempt to pull them toward me rather than toward him.

Dice 01 took one more pass with his cannons, making the Viet Cong (VC) take cover, before he had to head back to his base. I made contact with the F-4s as they were approaching, but they too were short on fuel and could give me only a couple of passes, which helped keep the VC in place. My command center reported that air rescue was still half an hour away, but another flight of fighter F-100s would be there in about 10 minutes. The VC were getting brave and making their way toward my decoy orbit location. I turned and fired a smoke rocket at them, which slowed them down but also made them mad, and they started concentrating their fire toward me. This at least kept them from looking for the downed airman. I did this a couple of times but ran out of rockets, and they began moving to where they thought the pilot was.

I fired back at them with my AR-14, which was a cut-down version of the M-16. The O-1 Bird Dog was

slow enough that I could open the side window and shoot out at them.

This again drew them back to concentrating on me and away from the pilot. About this time an Army helicopter contacted me and asked if he could help; he was very near the area, and I welcomed his help. I directed him around behind the downed pilot. From his hiding place behind the jungle area, he was able to pop over the jungle and set down right next to the downed pilot. The gunner in the chopper jumped out and assisted the pilot into the chopper.

The VC were taken completely by surprise, and it took them a short time to react. By then the chopper was beginning his takeoff, but before he could get over the tree line, he took several hits from the VC. He asked me to stay with him because he didn't know how far he could get before he had to put down. He made it about three miles away before he had to land. By that time air rescue arrived and picked everyone up. They also secured the downed helicopter, which was later returned to base.

It was a great day for all; everyone made it back safe and sound.

As a result of this rescue mission, the United States Air Force awarded me the Distinguished Flying Cross.

The citation of the award mentions that one of the reasons for the award was my devotion to duty. I believed in what I was doing, and I was devoted to it. As a United States Air Force officer I had taken an oath to defend my country; I was committed (devoted) to do the very best job I could.

Commitment is a word we are taught a lot about in the Church. When we are baptized, we commit to live the laws and commandments of our Heavenly Father. When we are asked to take a calling in the Church, we commit to do the very best we can at that calling. When we marry, we commit to be the best husband, father, and priesthood holder we can be. When we are committed and do the best job we can do, we gain trust, honor, courage, and respect from those around us. These are the attributes I strived for in the air force and with my Father in Heaven.

Following is the citation that accompanies the award of the Distinguished Flying Cross:

The Award of
The Distinguished Flying Cross
To
Oscar R. Adams

Captain Oscar R. Adams distinguished himself by extraordinary achievement while participating in aerial flight as a Forward Air Controller near Quan Loi, Republic of Vietnam, on 15 July 1967. On that date, the number two pilot of a flight of fighters controlled by Captain Adams ejected in hostile territory. Captain Adams started rescue proceedings and successfully coordinated the downed pilot's rescue from Viet Cong elements that had advanced to within 200 feet of his location. The instant grasp and absolute control of the situation that was exercised by Captain Adams definitely prevented the downed pilot from being killed or captured. The professional competence, aerial skill, and devotion to duty displayed by Captain Adams reflect great credit upon himself and the United States Air Force.

PILOT'S BIOGRAPHY

Rank and branch service: captain, United States Air Force

Call sign: Sidewinder

Hometown: Cedar City, Utah

Family: married to Lolene M. Adams; three children; seven grandchildren

Church callings: formerly served as counselor in bishopric, high priests group leader, and ward clerk; currently serves as bishop of singles ward at Southern Utah University

Current occupation: retired American Airlines captain

Hobbies: enjoyed serving with his wife in the Fiji Suva Mission; loves to spend time with grandchildren; golf, horses

Awards and recognitions: Silver Star, Distinguished Flying Cross, and Air Medals (14)

Oscar "Ron" Adams with the O-1 Bird Dog

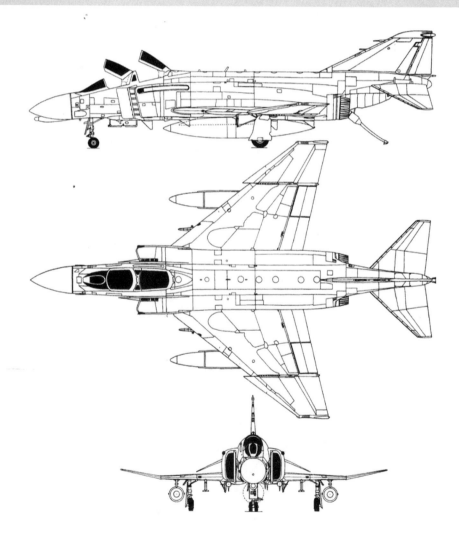

CHAPTER TWELVE

YOU NEVER KNOW WHEN SOMEONE IS LISTENING

WILLIAM SPENCER

I was a 29-year-old United States Air Force fighter pilot, hanging from a parachute, slowly descending into hostile territory. I looked below my dangling legs as I watched my doomed F-4 Phantom shudder, shake, and cartwheel its fiery way to the ground. Missing its tail section and a large part of the left wing, it was now totally engulfed in flames. It was hard to imagine I had been sitting in the cockpit, at the very center of the fireball, a few seconds before. Finally, I saw it hit the ground with a huge concussion that I could see but not hear. The fire and smoke reached into the sky several thousand feet. I thought for a few seconds how unlikely it was for a small-town Texas boy to be involved in such a monumental problem as this was turning into.

I had been hit by a heat-seeking missile from an unseen MiG-21. Now my survival training overcame

my shock, and I did a quick inventory of my physical condition and that of my equipment. My chute was fine, with only one or two blown panels, and my injuries were minor—a small cut in the right corner of my mouth from the bayonet on my oxygen mask that had come loose in the ejection. I looked above me, saw two F-4s circling, and reached for my survival radio to get out one last message before I became the newest prisoner of war in this long and complicated conflict called the Vietnam War. "This is Bass Zero Two Alpha. I'm in a chute. I'm A-OK. See you after the war." I wanted my family to know that I was in good physical condition and still had an optimistic outlook. I would be fine. I wanted my family to have this message to bear them up.

Now I shifted focus to the immediate problems. I was coming down in an area where I knew there would be no rescue attempt. I was drifting toward the ground into one of the most hostile and feared nations on the earth. I was on my own, and I would be either killed or captured by an enemy I knew to be ruthless.

I spent the next nine months held captive by the North Vietnamese. I was imprisoned primarily in the famous "Hanoi Hilton," but this story is not about that time. This story is about the time immediately before I was shot down. This story is about events that affected my life much more than being a POW, events that were much more profound, powerful, and life-changing than a heat-seeking missile or a raging fire in a dying aircraft.

A few months before I was shot down on July 5, 1972, I had been assigned a new roommate. Our squadron was housed with two pilots to each room, and we got to know each other pretty well. My new roommate was quite different from the typical fighter pilot. He didn't drink, smoke, use profanity, or display the arrogant swagger characteristic of most fighter pilots I knew. Lee was a young, friendly lieutenant who smiled a lot and had a genuine interest in others.

Although our schedules conflicted most of the time, we got to know each other quickly. I was very interested to learn that Lee was a member of The Church of Jesus Christ of Latter-day Saints. I had never known a Mormon before or really had a chance to learn about that faith. There was subtle pressure to conform to the common ways of doing things in our squadron, but Lee did not adjust his principles. I admired him for having the courage to conduct himself according to his beliefs. In the short time we had together, we discussed the subject of religion. I had been raised a Protestant and was intrigued by the simple way that Lee was able to discuss his religion. I learned that he had served a two-year mission for his church and was impressed by his sincere interest in explaining the principles of his faith. I learned of the First Vision and of the Prophet Joseph Smith. I remember that it seemed quite a tall tale to me at first. Lee also gave me a copy of the Book of Mormon and explained how he believed this book to be scripture, along with the Holy Bible. I had read about 30 pages in the book before I was shot down.

The most interesting thing about my discussions with Lee was the time he invited me to attend a "family home evening" with some of the other few members of the Church stationed at our base in Thailand. We met with this group of 10 or so members only once before I was shot down. Lee and I were the only officers in the group. The thing about this group that impressed me the most was the way they related to each other. There was no superficial military relationship to get in the way of true communication. In fact, they called each other "Brother." I felt the genuine feeling of love and concern they had for each other. I had never experienced that kind of relationship between officers and enlisted men to that degree before that time. It was unique, and it made a lasting, positive impression on me.

As a direct result of these positive feelings I had toward my experience with Lee and his "brothers," I joined the Church in 1976, some three years after being repatriated to this great nation. Two young missionaries knocked on my door when I was stationed in Florida, and as a result of the good feelings I had about what I had learned of the Church, I let them into my home. I did the simple things they asked me to do and finished reading the Book of Mormon on Christmas Day of that year. The testimony I gained from that first reading has never left me.

One of the greatest experiences of my life was on

June 26, 2000, as I rose out of the waters of baptism as proxy for my father, who had passed away. June 26 was his birthday, and I could not control my emotions as I felt his spirit accept this ordinance. Those in the baptismal font had to wait several minutes while I regained control of my emotions. Finally, I was able to share with them the feelings I had, the love I felt for my father, and the sure knowledge that he had just accepted this ordinance. I did not tell them how close all of this came to never happening, how close I had come to being destroyed by an enemy far away some 28 years before.

I completed the rest of my father's work that day in the Salt Lake Temple and have always been grateful for the incredible changes in my life that have resulted from that first introduction by my friend Lee to the greatest gift anyone could ever receive. How my life and the lives of my family have changed as a result of his concern and willingness to share the gospel with me and to risk rejection to reach out to a "brother"!

We should remember that you never know how a friend might react to your sincere testimony. You never know when a friend might truly feel the Spirit. You never know when someone is listening.

PILOT'S BIOGRAPHY

Rank and branch of service: lieutenant colonel, United States
Air Force, retired

Call sign: Spence

Hometown: Brownsville, Texas

Family: married to Davina E. Spencer; six children; six grandchildren

Church callings: formerly served as ward executive secretary,
Sunday School teacher, and in elders quorum and high
priests group leadership; currently serves as a Church
service missionary at the Family History Library in Salt
Lake City and as high priests group teacher

Current occupation: small business owner

Hobbies: family and Church activities, golf, Brigham Young
University football, and Utah Jazz basketball

Awards and recognitions: 92
combat missions in Viet-
nam; Distinguished Flying
Cross, Bronze Star with
one oak leaf cluster,
Purple Heart, Meritorious
Service Medal with one
oak leaf cluster, Air Medal
with six oak leaf clusters,
Air Force Commendation
Medal with one oak leaf
cluster, and Army Com-
mendation Medal

William Spencer with an F-16

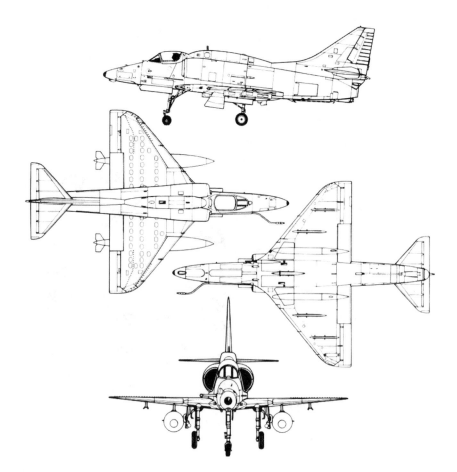

CHAPTER THIRTEEN

UNSAFE GEAR INDICATOR

THOMAS W. MCKNIGHT

I had been in Key West, Florida, for a week. Not a bad deal, except that I was finishing the last of my training in the A-4, the aircraft the United States Navy used at the time in advanced jet training. This was the final phase of jet training before I would receive my wings and be assigned a tactical aircraft. As I was a marine, this meant the AV-8B Harrier, A-6 Intruder, EA-6B Prowler, or the F/A-18 Hornet. The aircraft carrier *USS Lexington* was in the Gulf of Mexico, and several of us young student naval aviators were anxious to finish carrier qualification. This meant two "touch and go" landings and six "traps," or carrier landings, on the *Lexington* as it sailed ahead in the gulf.

A few days earlier I had completed my two touch-and-goes and four of my required six traps. On the last day the *Lexington* was to be in the area before it returned to Pensacola, I was up early to take off from Naval Air Station Key West. After an early briefing, while waiting for the sun to rise, I went to maintenance to see what jet I was assigned to fly out to the *Lexington*. When I found out, I also asked to look at the aircraft discrepancy book and see what maintenance had been performed on the jet in recent history.

To my surprise I saw that this jet had been out to the ship the day before but had returned because of an "unsafe" indication in the right main landing gear. Maintenance could not find the problem, so they signed off: "Drop checks good, aircraft checks 4.0 on deck." This was navy code for "we can't find the problem, so we can't fix the problem. Best of luck to the next pilot who flies this bucket of bolts." I took the remaining time to study possible scenarios and remedies in case the unsafe indication presented itself to me.

Just after the sun rose, I was over the *USS Lexington* and ready to complete my training. Unfortunately, as I attempted to lower my landing gear, the "unsafe" indication in the right main landing gear appeared. Another A-4 was directed to join up on me and check me over to see if the gear looked safe or not. My new wingman said, "It's unsafe." Next I was directed to raise the gear and return to Key West. It came up, and my wingman and I flew toward Key West.

The flight was about 15 minutes. In that 15 minutes, I prayed and reviewed corrective actions to my predicament and prayed some more. About 15 miles north of United States Naval Air Station Key West, my wingman and I began more troubleshooting and actions to try to correct my problem, all of which brought the same reply from my wingman: "Unsafe." As long as I could raise the gear, I had the option of landing with the gear up. If I could not raise my gear and had one of the main gear down and one up, there was only one option: eject. After trying, with no luck, to get my landing gear to work normally, it was time to return to land. I raised the gear handle, and it came up.

Air traffic control at Key West was holding all aircraft on the ground to allow me priority handling when I returned to the air station. I had been in radio contact with my base, which had a landing signal officer (pilots trained in bringing aircraft safely onto aircraft carriers) out by the runway on a radio to talk to me. They had formulated a game plan.

Base told me to fly a low, flat, practice approach to get the picture and then drop my tail hook and fly a low, flat approach to a gear-up arrested landing on the runway. I would actually land on the two large drop tanks attached to the underside of my wings. They were usually full of 1,000 pounds of fuel each, but now they were empty. I was surprised by the arrested landing part, but I trusted their judgment. Besides, a trap on the long runway was not as hard as a trap on the ship, where the angled deck is driving away from you and moving up and down. When I got abeam the runway, I told base I had only 600 pounds of fuel left (not a lot for an A-4). They told me "take a trap on the first pass."

One mile out I spotted the cable crossing the runway that was my target. There was only one; at the ship there were four. Shortly thereafter, I landed on the runway and caught the wire.

The fuel fumes in the "empty" drop tanks created quite a sight. As I landed on the drop tanks, the thin metal of the fuel tank ruptured underneath, and the escaping fuel fumes mixed with sparks from thin metal being scraped across the runway at over 110 miles per hour ignited two huge fireballs that quickly extinguished themselves as the fuel vapor burned. I shut down the engine as I was stopping and quickly got out while the fire trucks raced to spray foam under my A-4.

Normally, after an incident like that you are finished flying until investigations are completed and doctors consulted. In my case, I was whisked off to the hospital so they could take fluid samples and observe me. After two hours of hospital protocol, I was called by my squadron. The officer in charge (who happened to be my bishop) asked how I was feeling. I told him I felt fine. He then said that if I felt up to it they had arranged for me to fly back out to the *Lexington* in the next two hours to finish my training. If I did not go, it would take two more months to finish training.

I said yes. By the end of the day, I had my two traps on the *Lexington.* By the end of the month, I had my assignment: F/A-18 Hornets in Hawaii.

The Lord was with me. The old saying is "God is my copilot." I am not pompous enough to believe that. *He* led *me* that day. He was *my* guide. Studying maintenance books was not my habit back then. I was never nervous, never scared during the whole episode. I had peace. I knew I would be okay. I was God's wingman, and he led me safely home.

My prayer is that I will live my life in such a manner that on the Day of Judgment I can humbly say, "I was God's wingman, and he led me safely home."

PILOT'S BIOGRAPHY

Rank and branch of service: lieutenant colonel, United States
   Marine Corps Reserve

Call sign: Deacon

Hometown: Columbus, Ohio

Full-time mission: Nevada Las Vegas

Family: married to Elizabeth Kate McKnight; three children

Church callings: formerly served as a member of elders
   quorum presidency and instructor, Young Men's advisor,
   Primary teacher, and LDS group leader at Al Udeid Air
   Base; currently serves as ward Sunday School president

Current occupation: B747–400 pilot and instructor; recently
   served as a USMC liaison in Doha, Qatar; serves in the
   USMC as an emergency preparedness liaison officer

Military service: more than 3,000 hours in the A-4 Skyhawk,
   F/A-18 Hornet, and other military aircraft; adversary pilot
   in the F-5 Tiger II; mobilized to Iraq in 2005; several
   awards and decorations

Tom McKnight's A-4 after the belly landing at Key West, Florida
(note the arrester hook and cable)

O-1 BIRD DOG

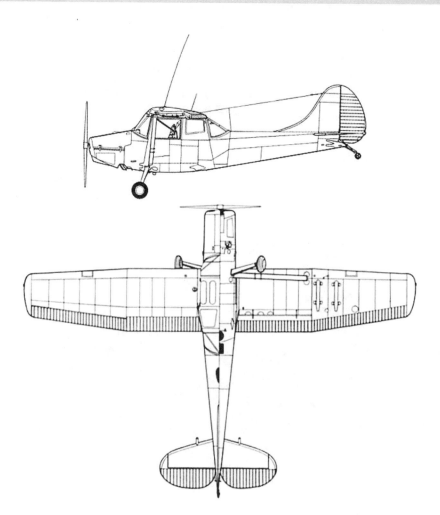

CHAPTER FOURTEEN

SILVER STAR

OSCAR R. "RON" ADAMS

In 1967 and 1968 I was a captain in the United States Air Force serving as a forward air controller (FAC) flying a single-engine spotter plane known as a O-1 Bird Dog. It was a simple aircraft, no sophisticated performance instruments, no exotic electronics or flight control systems, no radar transponders, just basic navigational instruments. It was open-window, seat-of-the-pants flying. We were taught early to fly at least 1,500 feet above the trees, which would keep us out of small arms fire, or else down on top of the trees, where the enemy would have a hard time getting a shot at us. We were never to fly straight and level if at all possible. We prayed that they had no big antiaircraft guns, which they did have occasionally in our area. When they did, it was like playing hide-and-seek: you tried to get them before they got you. The O-1 Bird Dogs were the link between the fighter bomber pilots and the ground combat forces.

Basically, the FAC's mission was to search out targets through visual reconnaissance or working with ground troops, find the enemy, and then direct the fighter bombers to them. The FACs were developed in response to a jungle environment in which fighters, especially jets, were too fast to see through the jungle canopy and identify targets. It was the FAC's job to know the area: He was assigned to cover and know where all the friendly forces were located. I was assigned to the First Infantry Division at Lai Khe, South Vietnam. Lai Khe is about 60 miles northwest of Saigon, near the Cambodian border.

On August 7, 1967, I was awakened at 1:00 A.M. by my radio operator. One of the Special Forces bases, Tong Le Chanh, was under attack, and air support was requested. I was airborne within about 15 minutes. En route to the target area, I was briefed on the situation and what had been ordered up to assist. The ground commander had reported that they were under heavy mortar attacks and frontal assaults, and things were going from bad to worse. They needed lots of help. My ground command post at Bien Hoa had already ordered up an AC-47 gunship, commonly known as Spooky. It could carry and drop lots of flares to light up the area, and it had three mini guns that could fire up to 6,000 rounds a minute. Two flights of F-100 and F-4 fighters had also been ordered up and would be in the area within 30 minutes.

Upon arriving at Tong Le Chanh, I made contact with the radio operator on the ground, and he briefed me on what was happening and where help was needed. A couple of army helicopter gun ships were the only aircraft available. We directed their fire to the north side of the camp where there was an open area

of about 300 yards around the camp that was covered with North Vietnamese troops (NVA) trying to get through the barbed-wire barricade. At this time Spooky arrived, and I directed him to where he should drop his flares. As I flew around these areas, I received a lot of small arms fire. I then detected a number of antiaircraft sites that had been set up to stop the air support.

The fighters showed up next. I briefed them on what we were facing, how to conduct their approaches and exits from the area, and what ordnance I wanted where. The ground commander and I felt that the most immediate need was to relieve the pressure on the north side of the camp, so that is where we put in the air strikes. With each pass the fighters and I received fire from the antiaircraft batteries. One of the fighters was hit with minor damage and had to return to his base.

More flights of fighters were being sent to help me. These new fighters began to suppress the ground fire, and with the napalm that the fighters carried, they put a fire wall between the enemy and the camp and drove the enemy back toward the jungle. There we used bombs on them to stop them from massing for another attack.

The battle lasted nearly three hours. In that time we

put in 12 groups of fighters and several army gun ships.
I was relieved of duty after three hours, as I was very
low on fuel and out of rockets. I returned to home base
to refuel and rearm and had just started to take a break
when word came that the FAC that replaced me had
received battle damage and needed to return to base.

I was immediately airborne and headed back to the
combat area. The sun was just coming up when I
arrived. We continued to drive the NVA troops back
and away from the Special Forces camp. Then I landed
at the camp and met with the soldiers and the camp
commander to see what more we could do to help. The
bravery and courage of these men was something I
shall never forget: More than a third of the defenders of
the camp had been injured or killed.

As I look back on these events and my time spent
in the United States Air Force, I know that the training I
received early in my life prepared me for what I had to
face in these combat situations. That early training
taught me courage, trust and honesty, of a life after
death, and of commitment to others. Many people put
their trust in me to do my job and help save their lives.
There were times that I could have withdrawn without
dishonor. But with the training I received, I pressed on.
Yes, I was afraid many times, but I was more afraid of

letting down those who had put their trust in me, even to the point of my dying for them.

Early on Sunday mornings, *Music and the Spoken Word* was rebroadcast on Armed Forces radio from Saigon, and I could receive it on my ADF radio receiver. I often volunteered to fly on Sunday mornings so I could listen to the broadcast of the Mormon Tabernacle Choir. It was a little touch of home and Church in the middle of the war zone. It was a spiritual uplift to get me through the week. I will always have a soft spot in my heart for this broadcast that kept me close to the gospel.

Following is the citation to accompany the award given me after the events recounted in this story:

The Silver Star

To: Oscar R. Adams

Captain Oscar R. Adams distinguished himself by gallantry in connection with military operations against an opposing armed force as a Forward Air Controller directing combat support missions at Tong Le Chanh Special Forces camp, Republic of Vietnam, on 7 August 1967. On that date, Captain Adams was scrambled from Lai Khe to provide air support for Tong Le Chanh, which was under heavy mortar attacks and frontal assaults. Captain Adams directed fighter aircraft, army gunship helicopters, and C-47 gun ships on anti-aircraft gun emplacements, mortar positions, and troop massing areas alleviating those hostile threats. Missions were also directed along the perimeter of the Special Forces camp to save the garrison from being overrun. Throughout the three hours Captain Adams was in the battle area, he was subjected to intense ground fire, cross fire, incoming and outgoing mortar rounds and ricocheting rounds from both the friendly and hostile forces. By his gallantry and devotion to duty, Captain Adams has reflected great credit upon himself and the United States Air Force.

PILOT'S BIOGRAPHY

Rank and branch service: captain, United States Air Force

Call sign: Sidewinder

Hometown: Cedar City, Utah

Family: married to Lolene M. Adams; three children; seven
 grandchildren

Church callings: formerly served as counselor in bishopric,
 high priests group leader, and ward clerk; currently serves
 as bishop of singles ward at Southern Utah University

Current occupation: retired American Airlines captain

Hobbies: golf, horses; enjoyed serving with his wife in the Fiji
 Suva Mission; loves to spend time with grandchildren

Awards and recognitions: Silver Star, Distinguished Flying
 Cross, Air Medals (14)

Oscar "Ron" Adams with the O-1 Bird Dog

F-18 HORNET

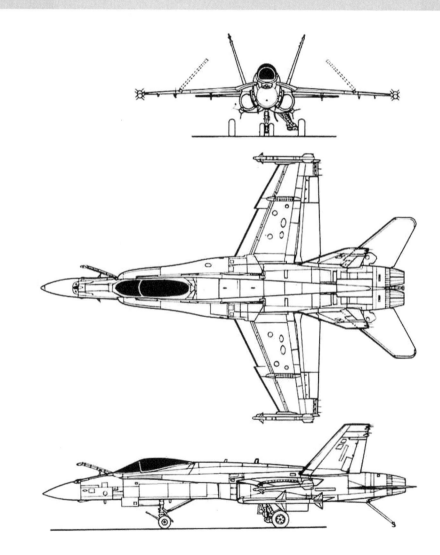

CHAPTER FIFTEEN

VERTIGO

THOMAS W. MCKNIGHT

During the winter of 1994 I was the number four F/A-18 of a flight of four. Three of my closest friends—Box, Boomer, and Gus—were one, two, and three respectively. Our squadron, the Death Angels, was based in Kaneohe, Hawaii. We were on a six-month rotation to Iwakuni, Japan. This flight was our third, and last, leg of the day. We had started in Iwakuni that morning, flying a low-level flight to Atsugi Naval Air Station just outside Tokyo. We got gas and a snack and then flew to Osan Air Base in Korea. The last leg was from Osan to Yakota Air Base on the outskirts of Tokyo. Our mission that day was officially Power Projection and routine training. Our real mission was from a much higher level and has only recently been declassified. We were each carrying handwritten orders from the highest level of command. Mine read roughly as follows. "More purses, another mink blanket, and any-thing cute you think I might like. Love, Liz."

Yes, all of us hard-charging, carnivorous, steel-bending marine fighter pilots were on a shopping trip for our wives. We had left our families in Kaneohe several months prior and were doing what we could to return the support we had been getting from home. We were in Japan flying F/A-18s, sleeping, and being housed and fed by the United States Marine Corps. Our wives were at home taking care of the kids, paying bills, and holding our homes and families together. Three hours of bargaining on the streets of Osan was a small price to pay to say thank you for all they were doing for our families. Our stop in Yakota was deliberate. Our marine accommodations were spartan compared with the luxurious accommodations the air force provided.

The day had been a success. Our classified mission came off without a hitch. As we got into our jets in Osan, I could feel a cold coming on. I was glad this would be our last leg. I could use a good night's sleep in some posh room in the air force bachelor officers' quarters (BOQ). As we took off and flew east to Tokyo, the sun was setting in the west. We were above the clouds, and the moon was coming up in the east. The weather in Tokyo was forecast to be cold with a high thin overcast.

We didn't think anything of it.

As the flight progressed, I got more tired and pictured myself in my cozy BOQ room. Flying over the Sea of Japan, we could see that the overcast layer appeared thicker than forecast, but it was more important to us to know where the base, or bottom, of the clouds was. The forecast called for the bottoms to be about 10,000 feet. When we got close enough to Yakota, Boomer switched off our flight common frequency in his number two radio to listen to the current weather broadcast at Yakota. (The number 1—comm 1—radio was for air traffic control. The number 2—comm 2—was used for interflight communications so we could talk to one another and pass information as needed.)

Boomer's voice came up on comm 2, telling us that the current weather was worse than forecast. The thin overcast was now thicker than we had thought. This meant that our four-ship formation would break up into two two-ship formations. Box would lead Boomer as they flew through the clouds, and Gus would lead me. Gus and I would fall back to several miles behind Box and Boomer. Tokyo air traffic control would guide each two-ship formation into Yakota. Boomer would fly very close formation on Box, and I would fly very close on Gus. This was normal and typically very easy in the F/A-18.

As we descended into the clouds, we saw that they were thicker than we had expected, so I flew closer to Gus. Our wings were overlapped, but my left wing was about five feet below his right wing. My canopy was about five feet from his right wingtip. If my flight lead was smooth and deliberate, all I had to do was maintain my sight picture on his aircraft. Gus was one of the best flight leads in the squadron, so I wasn't worried. We could hear air traffic control vectoring Box and Boomer around, so we knew we would get the same turns and descents that they did.

Tokyo instructed Gus to turn 90 degrees to the right and descend. Gus rapidly rolled right, and I was caught off guard. I had to roll just as quickly to avoid a collision. I rolled and stopped, but the rapid roll combined with the abrupt stop to maintain my sight picture on Gus's aircraft tricked my inner ear. My instruments told me we were in a shallow descent with our wings level; however, my body told me I was corkscrewing out of control. My inner ear recognized the rapid roll, but the combination of fatigue and the onset of a cold left my senses less than sharp and my inner ear did not recognize the stop of the roll.

I was in trouble! I had experienced the leans, a lesser version of this phenomenon, but this was full-blown vertigo, or spatial disorientation. It was rapidly getting worse.

The only way to fix the problem was to break out of the weather. We still had thousands of feet to descend before we would see the ground. I knew my condition was bad. I was in danger and because of my physiological state, I felt Gus was also in danger. I knew that a clear sky with clouds and a bright moon was only 5,000 feet above me.

My problem was that "above" had now become an issue. My body had no idea of what was up or down. I still felt I was in a violent corkscrew to the ground. I told Gus I had extreme vertigo and that I was going to separate from him and climb back on top of the clouds. I can't even remember if he said anything.

I remember moving away from him to the right. When I was sure I was separated from him, it took all I had and a quick prayer to get the nerve to perform my next task. I focused solely on my instruments, leveled my wings, and pulled back on the stick. I had to trust my instruments because my body told me I was upside down, pulling straight for the ground. My altimeter said I was climbing. My body disagreed. I pushed the throttles forward into afterburner. This would be over soon . . . one way or the other.

I remember almost everything about those few minutes: prayer and a reflection that my patriarchal blessing had said I would have children. Liz and I had none at the time. I was a worthy temple recommend holder so I had a glimmer of faith. That instant I shot out of the top of the clouds into the clear star- and moon-filled night.

My eyes now had the information they needed to communicate with my brain and override my inner ear. My world was instantly right side up. I had a brief moment of relief, and then I realized that what goes up *must* come down. I had to land, and soon. My fuel was not low, but it limited the options I had.

Then I heard Box call me on comm 2: "Deacon" (Deacon was my call sign from the first day my squadron learned I had served a mission for The Church of Jesus Christ of Latter-day Saints), "you will break out at 700 feet with great visibility."

I told Tokyo control I needed a long straight descent into Yakota. Luckily, they accommodated me. I was nervous but again I remembered my patriarchal blessing, and I knew my life was in order. With renewed confidence and greater faith, I once again descended into the clouds. Focused on the instruments and trusting them for a second time as never before, I broke out to the lights of the city with the runway right where I expected it to be. The landing was uneventful.

I shut down the airplane and sat alone in my dark, quiet cockpit. A prayer of thanks was in order. I sat for several minutes. Then the air force aircrew van pulled up next to my jet. Box, Boomer, and Gus were in the van waiting for me. When I got in, they all could tell I was shaken up by the experience. I had never been that disoriented in my life. Box said, "Deacon, you look as white as a ghost."

Gus said, "How ya' doin', buddy?"

"Not good," I responded.

He put his arm around me and said, "How about if we take you to the officer's club and buy you the biggest ice cream sundae we can find?"

I smiled. They knew me well.

As I have reflected on what happened that night, several lessons are obvious to me. For reasons seemingly beyond my immediate control, I found myself in serious trouble. The training I had received dictated that I put complete faith in my instruments. My mind and faith would have to overcome my body. I took control of my situation, and by means of prayer and faith, Heavenly Father guided me through. I am sure many of my decisions were influenced by promptings from the Holy Ghost. Liz and I now have three beautiful children.

My world has remained right side up. I am truly blessed.

PILOT'S BIOGRAPHY

Rank and branch of service: lieutenant colonel, United States
Marine Corps Reserve

Call sign: Deacon

Hometown: Columbus, Ohio

Full-time mission: Nevada Las Vegas

Family: married to Elizabeth Kate McKnight; three children

Church callings: formerly served as a member of elders
quorum presidency and instructor, Young Men's advisor,
Primary teacher, and LDS group leader at Al Udeid Air
Base; currently serves as ward Sunday School president

Current occupation: B747–400 pilot and instructor; recently
served as a USMC liaison in Doha, Qatar; serves in the
USMC as an emergency preparedness liaison officer

Military service: more than 3,000 hours in the A-4 Skyhawk,
F/A-18 Hornet, and other military aircraft; adversary pilot
in the F-5 Tiger II; mobilized to Iraq in 2005; several
awards and decorations

Tom McKnight

CHAPTER SIXTEEN

STAND IN YOUR PLACE AND TRUST GOD TO WATCH OVER YOU

DAVID STOCK

My flying story began in the fall of 1966 while I was serving as a missionary in the Northwestern States Mission of The Church of Jesus Christ of Latter-day Saints. As my release date approached, it was apparent that I would not be able to return to college with a draft deferment. The only options I had were to join the military service or be drafted. I was visiting with a member of the Church who was a United States Navy helicopter pilot, and he caused me to think about becoming a pilot myself. I had never considered this as something I wanted to do. Not long before this, my younger brother had been drafted and was serving as a crew chief on United States Army helicopters. He told me of a program the army had called "High School to Flight School," an opportunity to become a pilot without having a college degree. This sounded much better than being drafted, so I visited the Army recruiting office and learned the details of what was required to become a helicopter pilot. After much prayer, I felt this was the direction my life was to take for the next few years.

With the permission of my mission president, I began taking the tests and physical exams needed to qualify. They found that I was fully qualified, and I was told that the earliest date for induction into the training cycle to put me in a flight school slot was March 1967. That worked fine for me, because I was to be released from my mission at the end of November 1966, and those few months would give me time to adjust and get ready for the military.

Upon returning home and reporting to the draft board, I was informed that my draft date would probably come in January 1967. The fact that I was qualified to become a helicopter pilot did not mean I would not be drafted. The only way to avoid the draft was to join before I was called up. I had no control over this situation, so I turned it over to my Heavenly Father, and within days, my recruiter called to tell me a flight school slot was available if I could get to Seattle on December 9, 1966. This was my answer for how to avoid being drafted, so without much time to get ready,

I found myself going from the Lord's army to the United States Army.

The adventure began with completing basic training and entering flight school at Fort Wolters, Texas. There I met members of the Church who were helicopter pilots and who encouraged me to become the best I could be. I also learned about what helicopter pilots in Vietnam did. From that I developed the idea of being a medevac (short for medical evacuation) pilot and devote myself to saving lives of my fellow soldiers. It was a great plan, and I was very happy to think I could serve my country and not be involved in killing.

As flight school progressed, I did very well. The army "rewarded" the best of our class, and I was one of 20 selected to be trained to fly the new Cobra helicopter gunship. The Cobra was the first helicopter designed as an attack gunship. It had no purpose other than attack, and it was deadly effective.

When the army decides you are going to be "rewarded," they don't change their mind. I could not get the assignment changed. I was now faced with flying not medevac helicopters and saving lives but the Cobra, whose sole purpose was to kill enemy soldiers. Again I visited with members of the Church who were also soldiers and understood the difficult emotions of

coming to grips with the task of being the one to pull the trigger. After prayer and contemplation, I resolved to be like my hero, Captain Moroni, in being a very good soldier and yet not delight in shedding the blood of the enemy.

I was appointed a warrant officer and rotary wing aviator on December 15, 1967. When I began training in the Cobra, I was a natural for aerial gunnery, and I developed a skill for accuracy that, according to my instructors, very few pilots have. I became a part of the aircraft with an inner sense of how to maneuver; this skill would follow me for the rest of my career.

Upon completion of my training, I was scheduled to be deployed to Vietnam in March 1968. In preparation for this event, because I was the first of my father's sons to be sent into combat, we held a special family fast that all would be well and that I would return home safely. The answer to this fast was a very clear no! All of the adventure and thrill of what was ahead for me was gone; I was sure I would be brought home in a coffin. My flight school class of 252 had already lost more than 30 during the Tet offensive of 1968. I really did not want to die for my country, but I had been taught by my parents that freedom was not free and this was my duty. My farewell with my mother was the hardest thing I have ever experienced in my life. She believed it would be the last time she could put her arms around me and express her love. But she held her head high and sent me on my way.

I was assigned to Bravo company, 25th Aviation Battalion, 25th Infantry Division, at Cu Chi, Republic of Vietnam. Our call sign was Diamondheads, and we were the attack company. The unit did not even have any Cobras yet but were flying the Charlie model UH-1 (Huey) helicopters. Only two of us were newly trained

Cobra pilots; all the other gunship pilots had been in the country several months, flying slicks (unarmed troop and supply transport helicopters) to gain experience to become gunship pilots, which are harder to fly because of all the extra weight and external gun mounts.

But because we had to learn gunship tactics, I was assigned as a copilot to learn the techniques of flying underpowered, overweight helicopters into battle. Our primary mission was to wait on standby at our airfield until we were called out to support the ground troops in battle. We were reasonably certain every time we took off that someone was going to shoot real bullets at us. In the back of my mind was the thought, "I wonder if this is going to be the day I die?" After a bit of time, these thoughts submerged, and I became the skillful gunship pilot I was supposed to be.

An LDS servicemen's group was organized at Cu Chi, and I loved going to our meetings. It gave us a great spiritual uplift to get through each week, knowing we had brothers who were not hardened by the harsh influence of war. Because of my involvement in the Church and the fact that Pepsi was my strongest drink, I was soon given the nickname "Deacon," a name I still proudly go by at regimental reunions. It created many opportunities to talk about the gospel with my friends. My best friend, George, and I talked for hours about the plan of salvation. Those talks were to be the only opportunity he would have on this earth to learn about this wonderful plan.

One of the protection devices helicopter crew members wore was an armor-plated chest protector that we strapped on as vest-type carrier; we called them "chicken plates." I am not a big man, so I was issued a medium. One night I felt strongly prompted to get a bigger chicken plate. Being concerned about my safety, I took my old one to supply and got an extra large. It was heavy and awkward, but I felt safer with a little more to hide behind.

On May 15, 1968, while on a mission supporting an infantry unit, our aircraft was hit by enemy gunfire many times. The pilot was hit in both legs; I was hit in the left arm and right shoulder. One bullet from an AK-47 rifle hit me directly in the chest on the very edge of that extra-large chicken plate, which deflected the bullet into my arm instead of into my heart. The medium-sized chicken plate would not have covered the spot where I was hit. One gunner was hit by shrapnel in arms and legs. Only the crew chief was not wounded. In addition, the engine had been hit, and our helicopter was going down with only partial power and two wounded pilots, neither of whom could fly the aircraft alone. Between the two of us, we managed to finish our gun run and expend most of our ordnance before being forced to land a short distance away from the battle. Our wingman remained in the air and protected us until an element from the ground got to our landing site and secured the area. We were soon picked up by a medevac helicopter (the job I had wanted) and flown to the 25th medical hospital at Cu Chi.

As we were being moved from the helicopter to the triage room, a counselor in the LDS servicemen's group who was an orderly at the hospital walked by and saw me. It was his day off, but he immediately turned his full attention to me. First, he cut off my garments and took proper care of them. Then, after the doctors determined my wounds were not life-threatening and my surgery would wait, he said, "I will get someone to come help give you a blessing," and left. A short time later they returned, anointed me, and gave me a blessing. I had not shared the events of our family fast with anyone. The blessing was short, but I can still hear those words: "Brother Stock, your family asked the wrong question. All will not be well with you. You have been injured and will be again. We bless you that you will fully recover from these wounds and, further, that you will complete your tour of duty and return home to your family a complete and whole man."

What peace of mind came over me to know that my Heavenly Father loved me so much that he could tell strangers about wrong questions and give me the assurance of a good life yet ahead of me. (Too bad for the enemy. I was now indestructible!) I later learned that my parents were given the same assurance that I would not die in that faraway country and that I would return home when my tour was completed.

After a month in the hospital and convalescence

David Stock with the chicken plate (note the bullet marks below and to the right of the number 68)

165

center, I returned to the Diamondheads. During my recovery, eight of the promised Cobra attack helicopters finally arrived. They were waiting for me to get back so we could fly a full fire team (two aircraft). We still had only two Cobra-trained pilots in the unit, so with just over 150 hours of combat time, I was appointed an aircraft commander and told, "Learn fast, because you will be given your own fire team leader as soon as we get more Cobra pilots assigned." By late July we were assigned more Cobra pilots. I was given command of the Diamondhead 30 fire team and spent the rest of my tour as a fire team leader.

Although I was inexperienced in terms of combat flying time, I was blessed to excel at my job, but I also acquired a reputation as a bullet catcher. It seems I managed to get hit by enemy gunfire more often than most of the other pilots. Most of the time, however, we would bring the aircraft home, maintenance would patch them up, and we would be out again the next day. It was a time of building great love and brotherhood with the men I served with as we experienced the boredom of sitting around, waiting for something to happen, and in the next moment, the fear of flying into combat and being shot at.

As often as I could, I traded on-call time with one of

the other fire team leaders so I could attend sacrament meeting on Sundays. One of those Sundays while I was in sacrament meeting, the trade-off team leader was seriously injured in a midair collision. Miraculously, they fell into a swampy area, so they all survived the crash. The severe injuries cut his tour short, and to this day he still is partially disabled by his back injury. It would have been me if I had not traded and gone to sacrament meeting that day. Little promptings like that were a normal part of my life as I tried to live close to the Spirit to guide me through those tough days in Vietnam. I have often reflected on how close I felt to the Spirit during that time. I am very grateful to know my Heavenly Father was watching over me.

The fulfillment of my desire to be a lifesaving medevac pilot came in December 1968. During a mission supporting an infantry unit engaged in a terrible battle, we were notified that a critically injured soldier needed to be evacuated. We tried to escort the unarmed medevac helicopter, but it was shot down before it could get to the landing zone. A second medevac helicopter was also shot down while attempting to pick up the soldier. That day I was filling in for one of the other fire team leaders by flying an old UH-1 Huey gunship helicopter, not my usual Cobra. In the UH-1, we would have enough room to place the wounded soldier in our aircraft.

The ground unit was telling us, "If we don't get him out now, this soldier will die."

The crew agreed we would be able to get in, because we could defend our aircraft while landing. My wingman provided what cover he could, and we landed in the landing zone and picked up the soldier. In spite of our aircraft having been hit many times, we still had partial power and not one of us was even touched by a bullet. We took off and headed for Cu Chi with a badly damaged but still flying helicopter.

After evaluating our condition, I felt the helicopter was so badly damaged that we could not safely land at the small helipad at the hospital but would have to make an emergency landing on the paved runway. I informed the control tower of our intent and requested an ambulance to meet us and take the wounded soldier the last 500 yards to the hospital.

We did manage to land safely on the runway before the helicopter quit running. We later learned that the soldier survived and was sent back to the United States for further treatment. Our helicopter did not survive, however. It was so badly damaged that it never again took off. From the spot where we landed, it was loaded on a truck and shipped back to the States to be completely rebuilt.

The hand of the Lord was over us. There was not one scratch on a crew of four young men, who still remember and talk of what they call the miracle of what we did that day. We all received the Silver Star for that rescue. While the others may not fully understand, I know it was the guidance and protection of our Heavenly Father during that event that saw us through.

On December 24, 1968, I was on a search-and-destroy mission covering a team of observation helicopters when we found the enemy. He made his presence known by opening fire on my Cobra (remember, I was the bullet catcher), hitting me with multiple 51-caliber bullets. They hit the bottom of my aircraft, with rounds of gunfire coming up into the armored seat, tearing it loose and slamming my head into the canopy so hard it broke the Plexiglas and gave me a real headache. At first, I thought the headache was my only injury, but I soon realized I had fragments in both of my legs.

The bullets had broken the front pilot's controls so he could not fly the aircraft. I was forced to fly the Cobra from the backseat, even though my seat was almost on the floor and I could just see over the instrument panel. Other than that, the aircraft was still flying, so I fired all of my rockets into the enemy position so they couldn't harm anyone else. We made an emergency landing at the small outpost at Ta Nin. I spent Christmas Eve in the MASH hospital (mobile army surgical hospital) there. On Christmas Day my company commander came to award me my second Purple Heart and take me back to home base. What a Christmas! Best thing about it was that my wounds were only minor flesh wounds, and I was back flying after a couple of days.

The remainder of my tour was relatively uneventful. During my year in Vietnam, I formed friendships that are still strong today. Our Diamondhead reunions are joyful times as we tell stories and cry over our lost brothers with whom we shared life and death events. In the year I spent as a combat pilot, our company did not have one soldier killed. But two weeks after I left, B Company lost four of my brothers in arms, including my best friend, George, who were killed in a two-day-long battle.

I have often wondered if I had stayed, would my skills have saved the life of even one of them? I would like to have been there with them to try, but it is one of the unanswered questions I live with to this day. I miss them when the Diamondheads gather to remember all that we share.

Through all of these experiences, I came to know how important it is to trust in our Heavenly Father's desire and ability to watch over us and guide us as we learn to submit our lives to his care. This has served me well during the rest of my life, and I am often heard to say, "I wonder what the next chapter of my life will be?" I go forward, knowing my Heavenly Father is watching over me and knows who I am. It is my testimony that when we are righteously standing in our appointed place, even in the midst of bullets flying around us, God will watch over and protect us.

PILOT'S BIOGRAPHY

Rank and brance of service: major, United States Army, retired

Hometown: Farmington, New Mexico

Full-time mission: Northwestern States, 1964–66

Family: married to Gail Baker Stock; six children; five grand-children

Church callings: formerly served as bishop and high councilor; currently serves as ward Sunday School president

Current occupation: high school Junior Reserve Officer Training Corps (JROTC) instructor; pilot, sheriff's department

Awards and recognitions: more than 4,000 flying hours, including 1,027 combat hours and more than 1,000 instructor hours; awards include Silver Star, Distinguished Flying Cross (two), Purple Heart (two), Bronze Star, Air Medal with "V" device and 38 oak leaf clusters, Vietnamese Cross of Gallantry, Meritorious Service Medal, Army Commendation Medal, Vietnam Service Medal

David Stock with AH-1 Cobra

INDEX

Pages that feature an illustration or a photo are designated by italics.

A

A-4 Skyhawk, *128,* 129, *132, 135*

A-10 Thunderbolt II, *28,* 29, *32, 36*

Adams, Oscar R. "Ron": earns Distinguished Flying Cross, 111–18; photos of, *118, 144;* earns Silver Star, 137–44

Astronauts, 64–65, 75–84

B

Baptism, 116, 126

Beliefs, 124, 162–63. *See also* Missionary work

Bertelson, Gil, 61–73, *73*

Bingo fuel, 22, 113

Blessing, priesthood, 76, 164–65

Book of Mormon, 88, 124, 125

Briefing, 6, 96, 138

Brotherhood. *See* Fellowship

C

Callings, 116

Canopy, 100

Cessna, 2, 152

Chicken plate, 163

Christmas, 170

Church of Jesus Christ of Latter-day Saints, The: example of members of, 123–26; and servicemen's groups, 162, 164, 167. *See also* Missionary work

Clouds: flying formation in, 22–25, 41; impede rescue, 30–31; staying below, 39–41; hole in, 42–43;

vertigo in, 49, 150–54; in Rio de Janeiro, 56
Cobra helicopter, *156*, 157–72, *160, 172*
Cockpit, 100–101
Cold War, 61
Columbia, 75–84
Commitment, 116, 141
Contrails, 67–71
Conversion, 123–26
Courage, 116, 124, 141
Course correction, 35, 72

D

Danger, spiritual, 34–35
Death, 141, 161, 162
Debriefing, 70–71, 108
Decisions, 104
Derrick, Thales A. "Tad," 5–15, *15*, 95–109, *109*
Desert Storm, 32
Devotion, 116
Diamondheads, 161, 166, 170
Distinguished Flying Cross, 115–17
Draft, 157
Duty, 116, 161

E

Earth, 79
Ejection: over Mekong River, 9; considering, 43; over Viet Cong base camp, 112; and capture, 121
Espionage, 61–62
Example, 123–26

F

F-4 Phantom: drawings of, *54, 58, 86, 90, 120, 122;* in air shows, 55; in jungle battle, 87–92; explodes, 121
F9F Panther, *38,* 39, *42*
F-15 Eagle, *46,* 47–52, *50, 53*
F-16 Fighting Falcon, *viii*
F-18 Hornet, *146,* 147, *152*
F-86 Sabre, 47–48, *50*
F-100 Super Sabre: drawings of, *4, 11, 94, 102;* on combat mission, 5; used for training, 96; photograph of, *109*
Faith, 83, 153, 154
Family: homesick for, 79, 88; doing temple work for, 126; support from, 148; fasting as, 161, 164–65
Family home evening, 124–25
Fast, 161, 164–65
Fear, 20, 76, 166
Fellowship: and rescue, 34–35, 47–53; among Church members, 125, 164; among pilots, 166
Flight lead, 22–25, 35, 97
Flight school, 17–22, 159
Focus, 22–25, 72
Formation, 18–22, 51, 149–50
Forward air controller, 7, 30, 111, 137
Friendship. *See* Fellowship

INDEX

G

Garments, 164
Garner, William T., 39–45, *45*
Gospel, 142. *See also* Church
    of Jesus Christ of Latter-
    day Saints, The;
    Missionary work; Religion

H

"Hanoi Hilton," 123
Hansen, Ralph S., 29–36, *36*
Headings, 6
Heavenly Father: relationship
    with, 44; plan of, 72, 163;
    reliance on, 80, 134, 154,
    158, 171; acknowledging,
    83; protection of, 154,
    169; love of, 165
Helicopter, 12, 33, 115, 157–72
Hess, Jay C., 89, 92
Holy Ghost. *See* Spirit
Home teaching, 34
Honesty, 141
Honor, 116, 141
Humility, 21, 77
Hunt for Red October, The, 66

I

Injuries, 163–64, 167, 169
Instructors, 19–21, 95–97

J

Japan, 147–48
Jenkins, Ab, 95
Jesus Christ, statue of, 58

Jink, 6–7, 8
Johnson, Kelly, 62
Judgment, 134

K

Knot, 98
Korea, 39–44

L

L-19 Bird Dog, 7
Landing: through hole in
    clouds, 43–44; of
    powerless F-86, 51–52; in
    Rio de Janeiro, 58; of
    space shuttle, 80–81; with
    open canopy, 105–8; on
    drop tanks, 131–33; with
    vertigo, 153
Lowe, Tom, 6

M

Maintenance, 130
Marriage, 116, 148
McKnight, Thomas W., 2,
    129–35, 147–55
Medevac, 159, 164, 167
Mekong River, 9
Miracle: of hole in clouds,
    43–44; of insulation, 91; of
    chicken plate, 163; of
    uninjured rescuers, 169
Missiles, 62
Missionary work: importance
    of, 34; and foreign
    language, 56; among

roommates, 123–26; and draft, 157; by example, 162–63. *See also* Church of Jesus Christ of Latter-day Saints, The; Gospel; Religion

Mobile control, 103

Moon, Leonard, 55–59, *59,* 87–93, *93*

"Mormon Meteor," *15,* 95

Mormon Tabernacle Choir, 142

Moroni, 160

Mother, 161

Mountains, 30, 35, 41, 57

Music, 142

Music and the Spoken Word, 142

N

Nelson, David M., 17–26, *26,* 47–53, *53*

Norway, 65

O

O-1 Bird Dog: drawings of, *110, 114, 136, 139, 144;* helps in rescue, 111–15; provides air support, 137–41

P

Parker, John, 6, 8

Patriarchal blessing, 152

Peace, 57, 104, 165

Plan of salvation, 72, 163

Portuguese, 56

Powers, Gary, 61–62

Prayer: hurried, 10–11, 104; of gratitude, 12, 81–82, 108, 153; in bathroom, 32–33; in tight spot, 57–58; before going into space, 77; in space, 80; in Vietnam, 88, 91; answers to, 91, 161, 164–65; before landing, 131; during vertigo, 152; and contemplation, 160; and wrong questions, 164–65

Preparation, 76, 83, 141

Priesthood blessing, 76, 164–65

Prisoner of War, 89, 122–23

Promptings. *See* Spirit

Protection, 91, 163–65, 171

Q

Qualls, Tony, *36*

R

Radar, 51, 56

Regrets, 44

Religion, 124. *See also* Church of Jesus Christ of Latter-day Saints, The; Gospel; Missionary work

Rescue: of downed pilot, 12–13, 112–17; spiritual, 34–35; of pilot in powerless F-86, 47–53; no

hope of, 123; in gunship helicopter, 167–68
Respect, 116
Rio de Janeiro, 55–58

S

Sabbath, 6, 142, 167
Satan, 72
Scriptures, 79–80
Searfoss, Rick, 75–84, *84*
Second chance, 44
Silver Star, 142–43, 169
Smith, Joseph, 124
Soviet Union, 61–62
Spacecraft, 63–64. *See also* Space shuttle
Space shuttle, *74,* 75–83, *78, 80, 82*
Spatial disorientation. *See* Vertigo
Spencer, William, 121–27, *127*
Spirit: brings answers to prayers, 11; feeling, 126; and music, 142; prompts, 154, 163; in servicemen's meetings, 162; staying close to, 167
SR-71 Blackbird, *60,* 61–65, *69*
Stampf, Frank, *73*
Stock, David, 157–72, *165, 172*
Storms. *See* Clouds
Students, 19–21, 96–97
Submission, 171

T

T-37 Dragonfly, *16,* 17, *23*

Temple work, 126
Temptations, 72
Testimony, 77, 125, 126
Thunderbirds, 55
Training, 17–22, 129, 141, 159
Transmitter, 40–41
Trust, 116, 141

U

UH-I Huey, 12
USS Lexington, 129

V

Vertigo, 49, 150–54
Viet Cong, 6, 111, 113
Vietnam: rescue in, 5–14, 111–15; serviceman almost shot down in, 87; POW in, 121–23; battle in, 138–41; helicopter pilot in, 161–70

W

Weather. *See* Clouds
Wind, 101
Wingman: losing sight of, 23; losing contact with, 29; flying with, in clouds, 40; losing, 44; guided by, 50–51; warning of, 90, 130–31; God's, 134
Worthiness, 44